Kenneth Slack

George Bell

SCM PRESS LTD

334 00093 9

First published 1971
by SCM Press Ltd
56 Bloomsbury Street London

© *Kenneth Slack 1971*

Printed in Great Britain by
Billing & Sons Limited
Guildford and London

Contents

Author's Note

The time that proved available for the writing of this book was unavoidably brief. This makes my gratitude all the greater to those of my friends who responded to an urgent appeal for help in the undertaking. Their enrichment of the book ought to be visible at a number of points. I would especially mention Mr Edwin Barker, the Rev. Peter Bide, Dr Kathleen Bliss, the Bishop of Bristol (Dr Oliver Tomkins), the Reverend Adrian Carey, the Bishop of Chichester (Dr Roger Wilson), Dr A. C. Craig, Archbishop Lord Fisher of Lambeth, Dr Norman Goodall, Sir Kenneth Grubb, Canon Hugh Herklots, Bishop Leslie Hunter, Miss Janet Lacey, Dr R. C. Mackie, Miss Sigrid Morden, Canon David Paton, Dr Ernest Payne, Dr Harold Roberts, the Bishop of Rochester (Dr David Say), the Reverend B. R. H. Spaull and Dr R. D. Whitehorn.

Once again I am deeply indebted to my secretary, Winifred Weddell, for most willing and efficient help in many ways. I would also express my gratitude to the staff of the library of Sion College. Without their help and the availability of that splendidly comprehensive collection the work could not have been done.

Introduction

At three o'clock one morning in August 1957 I encountered George Bell, Bishop of Chichester, in the sordid surroundings of a strike-bound Idlewild Airport at New York. All buses were affected by the strike, and I wondered how I was to get to the city at that unattractive hour. Naturally a car had been sent to meet the Honorary President of the World Council of Churches. We were both bound for the central committee meeting at Yale, New Haven. Bishop Bell invited me to share his car.

As we drove that early morning through the suburbs of New York and past the garish signs of the used-car lots he began to speak to me of the autobiography that he hoped to write. Just a few weeks before that he had announced his resignation of his see. It was known that he had preserved a mass of materials covering his life since in early manhood he had been drawn into central church life as chaplain to Randall Davidson, Archbishop of Canterbury. Perhaps this was a natural activity for one who had written, in his two-volume life of Davidson, what has been generally acknowledged to be the greatest ecclesiastical biography of the century and one of the finest in any category. The writing of his autobiography was obviously going to be the major interest of his retirement (alongside his continuing service of the World Council of Churches).

He told me on that car journey that he was wondering whether to write an Anglican or an ecumenical autobiography. I was bold enough to urge him that it must be both, and I am still perplexed as to how the possibility of such a distinction came into his mind. I recall how eagerly I looked forward to that volume when it should appear, and how strange it seemed that he should be speaking to me of it, for – although a Free Churchman – since early manhood I had been inspired by Bell's *Randall Davidson*, which had evoked a deep interest in the world of ecclesiastical statesmanship and in the relationship between Christian leadership and the secular world.

In the event the autobiography was never to appear. He bade farewell to his diocese in the autumn of the year of our conversation. In the August of the following year I heard him preach his last sermon, at Odense in Denmark. A few weeks later he was dead.

The materials for the autobiography became available for a biography. Norman Sykes, Dean of Winchester and ecclesiastical historian, undertook the task; but he died leaving only some substantial fragments behind. The work was then undertaken and brought to successful conclusion by Canon Ronald C. D. Jasper. His *George Bell: Bishop of Chichester* was published by the Oxford University Press in 1967.

It was a strange irony that Canon Jasper had made his name as an ecclesiastical biographer by his admirable and most readable life of Arthur Cayley Headlam, sometime Bishop of Gloucester. The irony lay in the fact that Headlam had been himself a notable figure in the ecumenical movement on the Faith and Order side, but the most doughty and vociferous opponent of the creation of the World Council of Churches, of which Bell was to be the chief Anglican adornment. Moreover, the grounds on which Headlam opposed the creation of the Council – that the Churches and the ecumenical movement would thereby become embroiled in unseemly and inappropriate fashion in the controversies of international and national politics – were almost the very grounds on which Bell would have rested his advocacy of the creation of the Council. What Headlam feared, Bell believed to be necessary if the Churches were to be related seriously to the life of men and nations today.

At no point was this divergence more sharp than in regard to the German church struggle. Bell was the sustaining friend of the Confessing Church: Headlam was the leading Christian apologist in Britain for the German government.

With this interesting background of intimate knowledge of Headlam, Bell's official biographer produced a book that was excellent in its coverage of the wide range of Bell's interests, splendid in its documentation, and judicious in its opinions. The question nevertheless has remained in the mind of this reader (who has with enjoyment read and reread both volumes) whether the author felt an equal interest in Bell to that which is so manifest in his treatment of Headlam.

Partly we may account for this by the fact that Headlam was far more of a 'character', as the world understands that word. Dogmatic, rude, opinionative, intellectually arrogant – there was a dark side in Headlam to give the contrasts that make a biography fascinate. Bell was wise, gentle, shy and almost forbiddingly industrious. There was nothing about him to catch the public attention, and no idiosyncrasy of temperament to attract or repel.

The fact remains that Bell was a far more significant figure on the world scene and, as my first chapter will indicate, has attracted more and more interest in the years that have followed his death. Headlam (although almost twenty years older) became a bishop only six years before Bell. He now seems like a figure from a past age: Bell pointed prophetically to an age yet to be.

This short study will therefore concentrate upon the things that make him one of the most relevant Christian figures of our time. Those seeking a full biographical study will naturally turn to Canon Jasper's book, to which, not least for its documentation, I am obviously most deeply indebted. Within its limits this short book is, to make the distinction made by Bell himself in our conversation at the airport, 'ecumenical' rather than 'Anglican'. That does not mean that I am forgetting that his primary work for twenty-eight years was that of an Anglican diocesan bishop, and that before that he was successively chaplain at Lambeth and Dean of the mother church of the whole Anglican communion; but the chief interest of Bell to most people today is the wider Christian work he did from that base, and impelled by the convictions of that churchmanship.

During his lifetime George Bell symbolized for many in the fires of affliction the reality of the *Una Sancta*, the worldwide Christian fellowship that was unbroken by war and other human evil. In the years that have followed his death the significance and relevance of the witness he bore to a world still tragically divided is being increasingly realized by many. This book is written to strengthen that realization.

1 The Growth of a Reputation

A prevalent pattern may be observed regarding the public reputation of notable men. When they die there is a flurry of interest accompanied by somewhat inflationary obituary notices. This is followed by a long period of total neglect, or even by a radical reshaping of reputation under a barrage of criticism. There seems a resolute determination to cut the reputation 'down to size', and little or no restraint on the voicing of savage criticisms that were held in check during the subject's lifetime by the degree to which he had commanded public support.

The subject of this short book is a total exception to all this. His reputation has grown as the years have gone by since his death in 1958. The perspective given by the passing of time has enabled men to see the remarkable degree to which this Anglican bishop had perceived the obligations of Christian obedience in the mid-twentieth century, a perception which also pointed to the nature of that obedience in the decades to follow.

This establishment of reputation is primarily a British process. Informed Christians elsewhere in the world had little doubt during his lifetime that George Kennedy Allen Bell was one of the chief glories of the *Ecclesia Anglicana*. His tenure of the ancient see of Chichester had given its name a shining lustre wherever Christian men were concerned with compassion and the establishment of a divine fellowship which should transcend the tragic divisions and disorder of our times. His office as Honorary President of the World Council of Churches was not just the indication of the measure in which he had served that body, and the movements which had brought it into being, but of his standing as an international Christian leader.

Strangely, one way in which part of the general public became aware of the influence which Bell had exerted, and of the representative character which he had assumed, was his appearance in wholly fictitious guise in a play which excited high controversy. The controversy concerning Rolf Hochhuth's *Soldiers*[1] centred on the fitness or otherwise of the National Theatre staging a play which made the unfounded assertion that General Sikorski's death in an air crash was an assassination to which Winston Churchill was privy. But interest was also aroused by Hochhuth's use of Bell as the chief protagonist against Churchill in the final scene of the play, set in the apple orchard at Chequers, a garden which is intended by the author also to have symbolic meaning. His prefatory notes before this act begin with Bacon's words, '*God* Almightie *first planted* a Garden'.

So far as is known Churchill never met Bell in any more than a formal and ceremonial way. The author of the play admits that 'the meeting with the PRIME MINISTER probably only took part in our imagination'. The dramatic reasons for Hochhuth's choice of such a protagonist are clear. Bell by his speeches in the House of Lords, deploring the deliberate destruction of the residential zones of German cities by aerial bombardment, represented the most vigorous challenge being given by anyone right within the establishment to the government's military policy. This senior bishop could not be dismissed as a left-wing hothead, nor even placed in that niche of futile idealism that the British have carved out for the absolute pacifist. Bell was not a pacifist. Nor could he be dismissed as a 'German-lover'. Although he was deeply convinced that there was another

Germany than that of the Nazis, he had been alert to the vile danger that Hitler and his followers represented long before the majority of church leaders. He had discharged in the ecclesiastical sphere something of the pre-war role of Churchill himself in the secular. Like Churchill he had seen the vileness and morally retrogressive character of Nazism for what it was.

'GEORGE KENNEDY ALLEN BELL, Bishop of Chichester, was the British Fénelon', writes Hochhuth, while going on to exculpate Churchill from the implication of being like Fénelon's antagonist, Louis XIV. This is a grandiloquent statement refuted even within the preface, for Churchill was certainly less concerned about Bell's criticisms than Louis XIV was about Fénelon's.

Hochhuth also says that Bell 'as the leading figure of the Ecumenical Council at Geneva was the most celebrated of the British bishops'. Was this true? In what sense, and from whose point of view? At the time in which the play is set the embryonic World Council of Churches, whose constituting first assembly at Amsterdam was still three years away, was still reeling under the blow dealt to it by William Temple's death. It is no exaggeration to say that all other bishops in England appeared at first rather like foothills surrounding a high mountain which had catastrophically disappeared. At Amsterdam Bell was to prove a natural choice for the chairmanship of the all-important central committee; but that time was not yet.

Hochhuth here is writing both as a continental European (perhaps specifically as a German) and with the benefit of hindsight. Bishops like Fisher and Garbett were virtually unknown on the international scene; Bell, however little acclaimed as a notable figure by the British public, had been deeply involved for many years in international affairs and in the relations of the churches on the Continent. Moreover,

13

this German author writing in the mid-'sixties could see clearly the degree to which Bell stood above the rest of the English episcopate both in prophetic insight and in being valiant for truth. When Hochhuth wrote, it was clear that Bell was the greatest of the English bishops. It may be doubted whether this would have commanded universal assent even amongst knowledgable and discerning churchmen at the time in which he was portrayed within that play.

Hochhuth's play focused attention on the degree to which Bell had become involved during the war in the whole question of our relations with Germany. His speeches in the Lords attacking the obliteration policy of Sir Arthur Harris' Bomber Command, or the official government demand for unconditional surrender, in so far as they attracted public attention at the time, could be dismissed as impractical idealism. Here was a man, it could be suggested, who had failed to assess the vehemence of the reaction of a British civilian population that had survived the horror of nightly bombardment only to find itself subject to the daytime terror of V1s and V2s.

When, however, a book like David Irving's *Dresden* revealed what had in fact been done to that gloriously beautiful city, and – far worse – to its inhabitants, men were bound to begin to reassess the witness that Bell had borne. There has also been increasing evidence of the small degree to which such inhumanity did in fact contribute to the ending of the war. This has forced a reassessment of the confidence with which such a policy was advanced as realistic and opposition to it was dismissed as a weakening form of idealism.

In a far more dramatic way Bell's name has constantly appeared in regard to one of history's great 'might-have-beens' concerning the final issue of the last war. The intense interest that the Christian, and even the general, public has shown in the life and death of Dietrich Bonhoeffer has brought Bell into a fresh prominence. That prominence derives in part from the degree to which Bell is seen as the English 'father-in-God' to this young German, so superbly gifted intellectually and so supremely committed spiritually. No one can read either of the considerable biographies of Bonhoeffer which have now appeared in English[2] without realizing what Bell meant to Bonhoeffer throughout his mature life. It is in regard to one meeting between Bell and Bonhoeffer that the note of high drama in this biography appears.

The story will be told more fully in a later chapter of how Schönfeld, a German pastor engaged in ecumenical work in Geneva, and then Bonhoeffer (each with no knowledge of the other's visit), came to see Bell during a war-time visit to Stockholm to reveal to him the existence and character of a strong resistance movement in Germany. It commanded the support of some noted military leaders, but was above all based on Christian revulsion against the bestialities of the Nazi regime. The emissaries called for some indication by the British government that there would be a genuine differentiation of treatment between a Nazi Germany and one in which forces had arisen to overthrow Hitler and his followers. Without such an assurance there seemed little point in men running the appalling risks involved in seeking the overthrow of their country's government, let alone wrestling with the psychological problems of acting in ways which could be described as traitorous in time of war.

Bell conveyed the information to Anthony Eden and sought the assurance. None was forthcoming. It is easy to accuse the British government of myopia at this point. Certainly the correspondence would not begin to loom as large in Eden's mind as it did in Bell's. The government in 1942 had enormous problems on its mind. Again the original reluctance of the British to face war with Germany meant that, once the decision was made, there was little inclination to do any other than see it through to the bitter end. Peace-feelers of any kind were seen, we may imagine, as at worst trickery and at best temptation towards a weakening indulgence.

The fact remains that what Schönfeld and Bonhoeffer told Bell was true. The absence of British assurances did not hold back the German resistance from action. The Hitler Bomb Plot of 20 July 1944 failed in its objective, and was followed by an appalling blood-bath. Many of the names of those who then suffered had appeared in the conversations with Bell in Sweden in May 1942. There can be no doubt of the genuineness of the information which Bell conveyed to Eden on his return to this country. What the effect of a British assurance would have been can only be guessed. Would such an assurance have gained essential further support in Germany for the resistance? Would it have enabled the resistance to move more swiftly? Would it have been accompanied by clandestine material aid? And would such support, urgency and assistance have made the plot effective? We cannot tell. It is only a 'might-have-been'.

It is still that. Had Bell been able to persuade the British government through Eden to give such support and assurance to the resistance, which was of a more than embryonic character, it is at least possible that the war would have ended far earlier. This would not only have reduced the cost in human life and in material destruction: it might have enabled a swifter turning of conventional forces to end the war against the Japanese and thus the avoidance of the use of atomic bombs, whose shadow lies across the whole of the rest of our century. Perhaps as important, eastern Europe, or a great part of it, would have been delivered from Communist domination. Germany would not be a divided

16

country, and there would be no squalid wall bisecting Berlin.

Bell was more than the intermediary in the exchanges which represent this fantastic 'might-have-been'. Or, we may say, he was only the intermediary because he had already come to be the most trusted of British church leaders amongst those who had been bearing their Christian witness against totalitarianism. The story that our remaining pages have to tell will reveal that there was nothing accidental about Bell's centrality in this fascinating and almost heartbreaking episode. He was not an unknown figure caught up by chance in great events. He was told because he was trusted, and because Schönfeld and Bonhoeffer thought that he would both understand and believe what they had to say. His ability to understand and his worthiness of trust had been achieved by his sensitiveness and discernment during the 1930s.

There is one other way in which Bell's name has continually recurred in the years that have followed his death. It is a way that might seem, by contrast with the portrayal by Hochhuth or the Stockholm meeting of 1942, so domestically ecclesiastical as almost to be trivial. I refer to the question whether he, rather than Geoffrey Francis Fisher, should have been appointed to succeed William Temple, when that overtowering leader so suddenly died in 1944.

To move to consideration of such a question may seem to be moving from the front page news to the gossip column. Does not such a concern betray a lack of any sense of proportion? Here was a man concerned with the fate of millions of refugees, with the secret movements within a dark totalitarianism to seek its overthrow, with challenging methods of warfare which rained deliberate death upon men, women and children in their homes as a way of crushing the power, or perhaps rather the will, to wage war. Does it matter for one moment whether he was given ecclesiastical promotion?

Some of the interest may perhaps be dismissed as mere clerical 'shop'. There is nevertheless much more to it than that. There is genuine concern whether this was a grave example of the harm that can be done to Christ's church by a kind of establishment which places in the hands of the secular power the ability to choose who shall be the chief pastors within the Body of Christ. If it could be proved that Bell was passed over because he had angered Churchill by the challenge that he had given both to bombing policy and the demand for unconditional surrender, then it would be a major element in any indictment of the present nature of the establishment.

Such proof, by the very private nature of the system of appointments, is not available. In the final chapter of this book, in which an attempt is made to assess the man and his achievement, we shall return to this issue. The purpose in mentioning it now is to note how the constant recurrence of this question, chiefly in memoirs and articles, is strong evidence not so much of his standing in 1944 but of his present reputation. Looking back, it now seems clear that the Church of England possessed in the 1950s two leaders of international stature, William Temple and George Bell. The thought is therefore bound to arise: why did not one succeed the other?

Temple was, of course, such a man as is only produced once within a century if, indeed, as often as that. The superlative quality of his mind was matched by a power of lucid, ordered utterance that enabled him to say profound things in a remarkably simple way. Born to the episcopal purple, he yet possessed instinctive sympathy with the under-privileged and a firm will to seek the re-ordering of society on more equitable lines. He was manifestly a leader of the first rank, equipped philosophically and theologically, as in speech, temperament and personality, to exert immense influence across the whole range of the church's activity.

Bell was not a man of this power. Although he had a mind of great ability, and (as we shall see) a remarkably wide range of interests, it did not begin to match Temple's power and scope. His was not a personality which could capture a wider public and evoke the kind of response which students and working-men gave to Temple throughout his life, and which the public at large gave him in his all too brief time at Canterbury. Bell had no power to kindle men's interest through the spoken word. Hochhuth's words on him as a speaker are mistaken. 'BELL is a very experienced and and a very English orator. Anger makes him quiet, the excitement is in what he says, not the way he says it. He also knows what a member once said to Joseph Chamberlain after his fluent maiden speech: "The House would feel a lot easier if you could manage to stutter a little here and there." '[3] There was no such element of calculation in Bell's speaking. It was just not his forte to be interesting in that kind of way. There can be no doubt that this lessened his public impact.

But as the years have passed it has become ever clearer that George Bell stands beside William Temple not just as a great adornment of the Church of England, but as an ecumenical figure of the first rank. Bell saw to the heart of what was happening in our century and unremittingly called men to a very costly Christian obedience as they faced it. It is this that has so vastly enhanced his posthumous reputation. It is this that makes his witness so worthy of study. Events, far from invalidating it, or making it dated, have revealed its permanent relevance.

NOTES

1. Andre Deutsch 1968.
2. Mary Bosanquet, *Dietrich Bonhoeffer*, Hodder & Stoughton 1968; and Eberhard Bethge, *Dietrich Bonhoeffer*, Collins 1970. (It is interesting to note that the *Publisher's Note* which prefaces the latter book begins with a reference to Bell, and quotes his words, 'The man who really knows the inside story of the resistance movement that I was in touch with was Eberhard Bethge. He is writing a biography of Dietrich Bonhoeffer.')
3. *Soldiers*, p. 174.

2 The Influence of a Great Archbishop

George Kennedy Allen Bell was born in 1883 into just that substantial middle class which has supplied so much of the solid leadership of the Church of England in our century. He was also born into that period of national confidence which provided not a few with a sense of security which (perhaps unconsciously) was the strong base from which they bore their confident witness in more tumultuous days. Bell was eighteen before Queen Victoria died. Although the work for which he is now best remembered centres on the agonies of the second world war and its aftermath, his roots were in more firmly compacted soil.

Bell's father was a clergyman, and George was the eldest of nine children, a typical quiverful of the Victorian vicarage. The father had an almost Methodist penchant for changing the spheres of his work until he became vicar of Wimbledon. Here he stayed until his preferment to a residentiary canonry at Norwich in 1918. By this time George Bell was well launched on his own ecclesiastical career, but the peripatetic character of his father's early ministry certainly contributed to a good deal of change in the young George's early education.

Despite this, those powers of mental application which were to mark the whole of this life appeared early in his schooling. They were to contribute greatly to his power to carry the demands of such wide involvement in ecumenical life alongside the tasks of a considerable diocese. His very able mind was made immensely more effective by a habit of industry.

Westminster was his public school. He was a Queen's Scholar, and enjoyed the opportunity of this early sharing as a spectator in great events in church and state reflected in notable Abbey occasions.

From Westminster he went up to Christ Church, Oxford. Here he distinguished himself by winning the Newdigate Prize, annually awarded for an English poem. It did not presage the arrival of a new shining light in the constellation of English poetry; it did indicate the measure of his love for English literature. That love found expression in the opportunity of beginning to supervise, while still an undergraduate, the preparation of a series of inexpensive volumes of English poetry, and editing several in the series himself. Bell retained an excellent gift as a versifier, as is evidenced by the lines with which Canon Jasper prefaces each chapter of his biography. These were written by Bell as an amusing justification of his election to the dining club known as 'Nobody's Friends'. They are both witty and full of delicate literary allusions. Bell has appropriately provided, too, for several modern hymn books one of the finest ecumenical hymns, 'Christ is the King! O friends rejoice', sounding a vigorous summons to world-wide service and unity.

In addition to the prestige of winning the Newdigate he gained an expected first in Moderations. Possibly because of his deep involvement in literary pursuits, this was followed only by a second in Greats in 1905. Had this been the first that his tutor had expected of him it might have had a marked effect on his career. He seems always to have been clear that he would seek ordination and thus follow his father. It was not equally clear to him that the parochial sphere was necessarily where he would exercise his ministry. With a double first he might confidently have expected a fellowship. The second in Greats closed that door for the moment. He went to Wells Theological College to undertake his specific training for orders. Somewhat startlingly by today's standards, one year was considered sufficient theological and pastoral training to equip a man for lifelong exercise of his ministry. So in June 1907, Bell was ordained deacon in Ripon Cathedral to a title at Leeds parish church. This was to be Bell's sole experience of parish work, and indeed one of his few experiences of life north of the Trent. This world-travelling bishop was to be a very southern Englishman to the end of his days. That apparently unfortunate second in Greats was to open the door to experience of the day-to-day work of the ordinary English parson, and of a very different world from Wimbledon, Westminister and Oxford.

In a curious way, none the less, it remained a privileged world. Leeds parish church was an immensely strong centre of church life, large in staff and possessed of a national reputation for notable vicars who were able to recruit a carefully-picked team of curates. Bell, moreover, was granted the unusual privilege of being ordained to the priesthood after only one year of service, when the custom of the parish church has been to keep men in deacon's orders for two.

Privilege nevertheless meant preferment to very hard work, and work of a kind of which Bell had had no earlier experience. This was the day when the Sunday afternoon 'men's class' was a vigorous element in the well-worked parish, and in Leeds the numbers were so large that it had to be broken into separate divisions. Bell's alone numbered two hundred. Despite his shyness and an appearance of extreme youth, Bell was the effective leader of this body of men. He applied himself with such characteristic industry to his new and unfamiliar tasks, particularly in visiting the homes of the members of his part of the class, that his health became endangered for a time. It may be doubted whether the parochial ministry was the most appropriate sphere for his gifts and personality, but the experience of the three years in Leeds was a considerable gain. He now knew what the life of a great parish was like. He knew, moreover, a good deal more about the lives of ordinary men in an industrial society than his own background, or his later work, would have taught him. At Leeds his concern for social betterment was kindled. The future leader in the Life and Work side of the ecumenical movement saw in down-to-earth and practical terms what life in a great industrial city meant for most of its inhabitants. The lusher pastures of Sussex, where he was to exercise his long episcopal ministry, would not have given him this. Even there he firmly developed and maintained close relationships with the trade unions, not always in a fashion most likely to commend him to the overwhelmingly Tory population of his see.

But after three years at Leeds the fellowship which had eluded him when he took his degree was offered him. His own college offered him a clerical studentship (i.e. a fellowship, to use the nomenclature of other colleges). To Christ Church he therefore returned in 1910, bringing with him the vehement social concern born of the Leeds experience, and becoming involved in a whole range of social enterprises. These were sometimes a little naïvely idealistic, but sometimes, as with his close concern with the university settlement movement, they were related to a very practical concern, in that case to engage the more privileged section of society in the direct service of the least privileged. It was in this latter work that he made his first acquaintance with one who was to be a colleague and critical friend in the House of Lords during the Second World War, Lord Woolton. F. J. Marquis, as he was then, was at that time the pioneering warden of the settlement established by the University of Liverpool.

Bell's recall to Oxford was not to prove the beginning of a long academic career, with the Leeds curacy receding to be an unrelated incident in a life devoted to quite different tasks. In 1914 there came the call to that work which was to mould the rest of his life of service to the Church of God. It was a call to serve the man who was ever afterwards to exercise the most profound influence on Bell's life and action. He was invited to be junior chaplain to Randall Davidson, who had already been Archbishop of Canterbury for eleven years.

The circumstances of the offer of this work were dramatic enough. He went to Lambeth Palace to stay with the Davidsons on the actual night on which war was declared, and found himself thrown immediately into the preparation of the prayers for the armed forces which the Privy Council had ordered to be prepared and despatched to every incumbent. A letter to a friend revealed the degree to which he was reluctant to make the move to Lambeth. His time at Christ Church had been very brief. Although fond of persons, his shyness made the thought of the social entertaining, such as must be involved in so public a life, unattractive. The growth of his social concern seemed a curious prelude to moving to the very centre of the ecclesiastical establishment. (One caustic friend, when the appointment was announced, mixed affectionate railery with reproach: 'Off to courts and palaces, is it, you are? This is monstrous flagrant treachery to the Working Man, supposed, wrongly alas, to be the apple of your eye!'[1])

All the friends whom he consulted, including some senior men like Bishop Gore and Bishop Talbot, were clear that he must go; and, despite his expressed hesitations, the letter which he wrote at the time revealed the attraction that

25

he had felt towards Randall Davidson. 'I like the Archbishop immensely: he is a quiet, simple, religious man, though he is also very able.'[2]

He was in fact extremely well equipped for the work which he now began. The junior nature of the post endured but briefly. The senior chaplain, J. V. Macmillan, left during 1915 to become an army chaplain. Thereafter, for fully nine years Bell was the Archbishop's alter ego, trusted by him with ever-increasing responsibilities in almost the whole range of concerns which centred upon, or crowded in on, Lambeth. The work was tremendously taxing, perhaps most of all in the opening years which were the years of war. But it was not exhausting in the fashion of the three years of unfamiliar tasks at Leeds. The work at Lambeth harnessed the particular skills which marked the mind and personality of Bell to the end.

He was not by nature a scholar or academic, ready to pursue the deep but narrow range of one particular discipline, but his mind was truly scholarly in the more general sense. His academic training had produced both a disciplined mind and one which knew how to tackle an unfamiliar subject and master it. (It was the same training as traditionally produced the great civil servant, and Bell was the supreme example of the ecclesiastical civil servant, using that phrase in a firmly non-pejorative sense). Given a subject to explore by the Archbishop, he could master all details, extract what was essential and do all the necessary preparatory work to relieve the Archbishop of drudgery and detail while enabling him to bring his wisdom and experience to bear upon a realistic assessment of the position.

Again, Bell's personality and temperament were well suited to the demands of the unusual position of a trusted Lambeth chaplain. There was nothing of extravert self-assertion about him, likely to arouse the irritation and worse of those who saw a young man posturing as an influential figure on the basis of serving the occupant of high office. His shyness and somewhat self-effacing nature delivered him from most of the accusations which readily fall on one who has moved to the centre of influence in young manhood. There was no marked thrust of ambition about him. Even his great chief, Davidson, who had occupied Bell's position in relation to Archbishop Tait, had not been immune from the kind of sharp criticism which expressed itself in references to him as 'Master Davidson'. He had been found at times to be a little too probing in his approach to his seniors, a little too open in his enjoyment of being at the centre of affairs.

Shyness, however, was not the evidence of weakness. Bell, even in those days as a chaplain, was not lacking in the tenacity of purpose which his later critics were too readily to describe as obstinacy. It was the tenacity of the representative of another, whose viewpoint must be maintained; but it was also perhaps temperamental. It went along with his power to master a subject. Having mastered it, and made his judgment, it was not lightly to be set aside. Only the presentation of a new set of facts, somehow unaccountably overlooked in his study of the subject, would be likely to loosen the grip of that tenacity.

The office of senior chaplain to an Archbishop of Canterbury in the modern era has become at least potentially one of very great influence. It was for Randall Davidson himself in a real sense the road to the Primacy. It brought him into close relationship with Queen Victoria (somewhat characteristically due to her concern with death-beds, for Davidson, as Tait's son-in-law as well as chaplain, had to supply details of the passing of the Primate and greatly impressed the Queen – an incident equally eloquent of her sentimentality and her shrewdness). The deanery of Windsor and the bishoprics of Rochester and Winchester were to lead Davidson back to the Lambeth that he had served as chaplain. Bell's own successor, Mervyn Haigh, went straight from the chaplaincy to be Bishop of Coventry, not without a little chagrin on the part of his chief, Cosmo Lang (not himself a stranger to rapid promotion).[3]

Much obviously depends on the calibre of the man who holds the post; but, equally, much depends on the man who is Archbishop. Should the Archbishop be reluctant to delegate, and be temperamentally unable to use the full gifts of the younger man serving him, the chaplain could readily be frustrated. The abler he was the more frustrated he would be. But where the Archbishop has the gifts of delegation and trust, and the chaplain the ability to respond to larger and larger demands, the office of senior chaplain can absorb all that any man has it in him to give. He becomes in fact the permanent under-secretary to a minister who is never out of office. All that is wrong with this analogy is that it implies what has never existed, a staff adequate to deal with the intensely varied subjects and the never-ending pressures with which Lambeth has to contend.

Davidson in his dealings with Bell showed from the first a willingness to hand things over to him and to trust him. This in a very short while transformed Bell's position from that of a junior Oxford don to a key figure in English church life, albeit one who did not himself occupy the public stage. It was understood from the time that he took up his appointment that he would shortly succeed Macmillan in the senior post, and therefore he was never restricted to the diocesan affairs which are traditionally the main concern of the junior chaplain. He found himself plunged into the whole work of a Lambeth facing all the questions which confronted the church in time of war. His conscientiousness and industry threatened to overwhelm him with work, but he can have had little doubt that he had come into his kingdom for such a time as that.

What manner of man was it that Bell served in this formative decade of his own life? Most of the picture that we possess comes from Bell's own work, the great two-volume *Randall Davidson* which, as has been remarked earlier, set a new standard for ecclesiastical biography. In it Bell fully repaid the trust and affection that he had enjoyed, for he gave to Davidson's achievement as durable and as fascinatingly readable a record as any man could desire for himself. But Davidson, who occupied the primacy for twenty-five years, and before that was an exceedingly influential figure in church life, and – in a measure – in secular life, is also naturally pictured in many of the memoirs of the period.

One aspect of the picture that emerges is that Davidson was possessed in many ways of an intensely *lay* mind. He had none of the detailed ecclesiastical interests, antiquarian, linguistic, aesthetic, of that ardent-spirited predecessor and friend, Edward White Benson. He was not a churchman in the way that his close colleague and successor, Cosmo Lang, was a churchman, with a mind which was clerical through and through. He was not a philosophic theologian like William Temple, son of his own immediate predecessor at Canterbury, and later (all too briefly) to succeed to the see himself. Davidson had an intense interest in and enjoyment of public affairs, by no means restricted to those likely to impinge upon church questions, or even those raising obvious large moral issues. When Bell's biography of Davidson appeared Bishop Mandell Creighton's son-in-law, Dr Cyril Bailey, expressed himself shocked at the worldliness of Davidson's interests (and Creighton himself would scarcely serve as the model for a withdrawn piety).[4]

Part of this dominant aspect of Davidson's interests arose, no doubt, from his early association with Tait, himself deeply involved (after the fashion of a Victorian primate) in secular and political life. Part arose from that Scottish inheritance that he shared with Tait. Part arose from his coming to be in early manhood the confident and adviser of Queen Victoria, with its inevitable involvement in matters of state. A good deal, none the less, came from the natural interests of his own mind.

It is unwise, too, to limit explanation to Davidson's natural interest and actual experience. His conception of his ministry was entirely consonant with the insights given by that Victorian theologian, Frederick Denison Maurice, whose work has been found to be seminal for much present-day thinking. Davidson was concerned with the world as the area of God's Kingdom, and firmly resisted any attempt to restrict Christian concern to ecclesiastical questions. It was a concept of duty as well as a temperamental inclination which led Davidson to be so deeply engaged in secular life. So in August 1918 we find him writing:

> I have been in pretty close touch with prominent actors and thinkers who have been handling English affairs and policy. . . . I have also had my ears open in the House of Lords, where I have attended with great regularity, and in the House of Commons when important things were under debate. All this results in my finding myself abreast of conversations among public men, when I am present at such, and on a good many points I think I have perhaps a wider knowledge than many with whom I converse, even though they be officials with access to Government information.[5]

All this had a profound influence on Bell. He was in many ways more firmly a churchman than Davidson, having been more fully influenced, along with most of the ablest Anglicans of his generation, by the Catholic movement. But he learned from Davidson the obligation of a Christian leader to be involved with the men who made the decisions affecting men's lives. He learned from him the value of the House of Lords as a platform for Christian leadership. Above all, he learned from him the widest possible conception of a Christian's concern with the common life.

There were, of course, obvious dangers in the way of leadership which Davidson chose. He had earlier been dismissed by some critics as too much the courtier. This was a criticism which did not survive the revelation of the manifest power that he brought to the primacy. (It was to be obliterated when Bell's Life revealed the courage of Davidson, as Dean of Windsor, when only thirty-five years of age, in restraining the Queen from publishing a further volume of her embarrassing *Leaves from the Journal of a Life in the Highlands*). But Scott Holland put his finger on the real danger when he said that Davidson's real danger was not the court, amidst the slippery places of which he had moved with safety, but old gentlemen at the Athenaeum who would lead him on one side and tell him what the great British public would not stand. An Archbishop who numbered four prime ministers, Rosebery, Balfour, Campbell-Bannerman and Asquith, amongst his real friends might be said to be in a position to exert a Christian influence in the places of power: he could equally be said to be very open to influence the other way, to a restraint upon the essential prophetic stance of the Christian leader.

Bell must have had an intimate opportunity to assess the gains and losses of Davidson's secular engagement. The losses were certainly minimized by Davidson's quiet and simple faith. He was above all else a man of integrity, and in time of war, when not a few Christian leaders were overcome by the prevalent hysteria, that integrity remained. The firmness of his dealings with Asquith over the publication of untrue statements under government authority,[6] the vehemence of his protest to the same premier on the

31

proposal to use poison gas,[7] and – significant for his chaplain's eventual stand in the second world war – his rejection of proposed reprisals for Zeppelin raids by bombing civilians,[8] may stand as eloquent evidence of the degree to which neither the Athenaeum nor an open door at 10 Downing Street had corrupted him. His quiet but unyielding opposition to a policy of reprisals and the spirit of hate continued to the end of the bitter struggle. He took the opportunity of the fourth anniversary of the declaration of war, preaching in St Margaret's, Westminster, to the King and Queen and both Houses of Parliament, to say:

> There is . . . a form of wrath which may degenerate into a poisonous hatred, running right counter to the principles of a Christian's creed, right counter to what was taught us by the Lord Christ, and which, once its roots get a firm place in our lives, may do worse than weaken, worse than coarsen and lower our high aims: it may corrupt and defile them with a horrid miasma, transforming what was a righteous – yes, a wholesome – wrath against wrong into a sour and envenomed hatred of whole sections of our fellow-men. That peril is not mere vague possibility. It exists. Such a spirit has, here and there, found voice among the sons of men in these years of strain and sorrow. As pledged disciples of a living Lord and Master who died upon the Cross for all who hated Him, we have to see to it that the spirit of hate finds no nurture in our hearts.[9]

The Christian leader who could speak those words on such an occasion had not suffered too grave a moral injury from his engagement with the secular leadership of the nation. The lasting effect of such a stand upon the thirty-five year old chaplain who then served him will be revealed in much of the later part of this book.

Even Bell's war-time chaplaincy was not unrelieved work and contact with great events. His own personal life knew both sorrow and a joy that was to abide until the end of his days. Within four days in April 1918 he heard that two of his brothers were missing, and the following month revealed that they had been killed. (It may have been this, and the long death-roll both of his contemporaries and his pupils at Oxford, that led to the support he was surprisingly to give to the Munich settlement in 1938: Bell, like many others of his generation, could never forget the decimation of a generation that had carried away so many of his brothers and friends.)

The joy had come a year earlier when he fell in love with Henrietta Livingstone. It was a love fully reciprocated, and they were married by Archbishop Davidson in January 1918, and lived happily ever after. The cliché has the fullest possible content. Hetty Bell was to share at every point the commitments and enthusiasms of her gifted husband. She was no doubt to suffer from being married to a man so conscientiously devoted to so many demanding causes, and so unremitting in his industry for them; but this degree of loneliness – unrelieved by the gift of children which was denied them – she gladly accepted for love of her 'George' and to advance work in which she believed as deeply as he did. No one who saw them in the closing years of their life together could doubt that each had given to the other great draughts from inexhaustible wells of sustaining affection. When Bell was called in war-time to tread somewhat lonely paths of misunderstanding and sharp opposition he had the warm security of that central relationship to uphold him.

Mild martyrdom in the cause of continuing burdens of administration and great affairs was Mrs Bell's lot from the very beginning. It was natural that his impending marriage should raise the question of his leaving Lambeth for independent work elsewhere (although Davidson had himself stayed on as a married man, with the added complication of having married one of the Archbishop's daughters). The importance of the positions offered to him, or for which he was seriously considered, revealed the assessment made by

B

the knowledgable of his gifts and his probable future. His name was seriously considered for two Australian arch-bishoprics and he was twice offered St Michael's, Coventry (now Coventry Cathedral) between 1917 and 1923.

With the extra burdens on Lambeth caused by war, and the place he had come to have there, a move until the war ended seemed unjustifiable. Then in 1920 came the Lambeth Conference of bishops, in which as assistant secretary he had a notable part. After that the question of a move was bound to be fairly constantly before both him and the Archbishop. Davidson's comment in a letter to Bell on the offer of one important living may be quoted:

> You and I have for all these tempestuous years worked together, and it is our joint work, and not *my* work in any narrower sense, which has had such degree of effectiveness as belongs to it. Take away one of the partners in the work and it is quite obvious that the doing of it would either not be done at all or done in quite a different way. . . . Next, you have by sheer effectiveness and resourcefulness of work, got into a position in central Church affairs which is markedly your own.
> . . . If you were a bachelor I think I should be ready to take the responsibility of saying that the central work at Lambeth is so important and your place in it so outstanding, that you ought to stay on here while you and I can still work together.[10]

That this is a generous assessment of Bell's contribution is plain: but it is also the expression of a man who was above all else respected for cautious judgment and deep wisdom. As such it is striking. Part of Davidson's greatness was his power to evoke outstanding service. (It was to appear in his partnership with Haigh, who began in highly critical fashion, even in the last years of his tenure of the see.) But such service can only be evoked if the latent powers are there. The perspective of history and later achievement now enable us to see clearly that they were there in the quiet young don whom Davidson recruited from Christ Church. By the time his apprenticeship with Davidson ended, after a decade of partnership between the old leader and his young chaplain, Bell was already emerging as a Christian leader in his own right.

By 1924 it was clear that Davidson had to part with him, but rarely can such an ecclesiastical parting have been such sweet sorrow. Ramsey Macdonald, exercising the first right of ecclesiastical patronage to be wielded by a Socialist prime minister, nominated Bell to the deanery of Canterbury. Thus Davidson lost Bell as his chaplain, only to gain him as dean of the mother church of the Anglican communion, where stood the throne of the Archbishops of Canterbury. Dean Wace, Bell's predecessor, had recently died at the age of eighty-seven. Bell was only forty-one, and young-looking for his age. To his new work he brought the maturity in still young manhood which had come to him through the ten years at Lambeth, which (together with his intense interest in the arts) made his brief time at Canterbury a time of rare stimulus at many points of the cathedral's life.

This was marked in the field of religious drama, and even if Bell had done nothing else he would have earned his niche in history for having created the conditions which caused the most influential poet of the period, T. S. Eliot, to enter that field, and to contribute greatly to the revival of verse drama. The first great undertaking during Bell's time at Canterbury was the commissioning of a play from John Masefield, *The Coming of Christ*, with music by Gustav Holst. It was performed before great crowds in 1928, and marked the beginning of a great movement of religious drama which has continued ever since. There had been earlier revival of the medium in the years immediately preceding, but Bell's act in commissioning a special work by a poet of such established reputation and a musician of equal fame, for performance in England's mother cathedral, gave great impetus to the revival. Offerings taken during the

35

performances were used to commission further new plays. T. S. Eliot's *Murder in the Cathedral* was the first-fruit of this forward-looking act. It must have afforded particular satisfaction to Bell that his initiative had led to the writing of one of the great poetic works of our century.

Bell's interest in religious drama was a lifelong one, and was the subject of his last speech in the Upper House of the Convocation of Canterbury. It was only part of his deep concern that the church and the arts should enter once again into fruitful relationships. The way did not always prove easy, as Canon Jasper reveals in his excellent chapter on 'The Church and the Arts'. The creative artist does not easily fit into the framework of permissions felt necessary to guard parish churches from permanent additions of an unworthy character. On one occasion Bell, when a bishop, took the unusual but perfectly legal step of sitting as his own Chancellor to give permission for a mural to be executed by the refugee artist Hans Feibusch in a parish church at Goring-by-Sea. Even more personal was the shock given by the unveiling of the portrait of him presented by the diocese of Chichester to mark his silver jubilee as its bishop. Bell had himself chosen the artist, William Coldstream, Slade Professor of Fine Art in University College, London. His aim undoubtedly was to secure a work of art, rather than the representational portrait more likely to commend itself to the subscribers. The portrait when it was unveiled did not show the rubicund pink face of their still rather boyish-looking bishop; rather they saw an almost Hindenburg-like figure of stern and teutonic ruthlessness. This certainly was no photography in oils; it was a work of interpretation. Some could have been found who would not have disagreed with the interpretation given, and Bell's official biographer records his own rather whimsical comment; 'It does represent a not completely absent side of my character.'

This action, despite its aftermath (when another portrait painter, at Professor Coldstream's own suggestion, produced another portrait more on the expected lines), represented Bell's sturdy lifelong determination to trust the creative artist. For him the arts were not a decoration of life, but a great part of its true meaning. Dr Robert Mackie, a colleague of Bell in the refugee work of the World Council of Churches, wrote that 'He did not labour to introduce the two worlds to one another; he was at home in both and wished everyone to be so.'[10]

When he was charged as Dean of Canterbury with the great enthronement service for Davidson's successor, Cosmo Lang, it was quite natural for Bell to include a procession of the arts. Lang wrote of this:

> The Dean . . . had taken infinite pains about all the arrangements. He had given full play to his vivid imagination in order to make the ceremony symbolic not only of ecclesiastical life, but of the national life, including 'the Arts'. Hence the series of independent processions, admirably marshalled. Never certainly had any previous Archbishop been enthroned on a scale of such colourful and symbolic magnificence.[12]

It would be the ceremony and the magnificence that appealed to the romantic and the prelatical in Lang in equal measure: for Bell it was that the realms of beauty, truth and goodness were inseparable, and were our experience of the divine. Bell was not only ecumenical in seeking the unity of Christ's people throughout the *oikoumene*, the whole inhabited earth; he was ecumenical in having found the unity of all human experiences of the divine, and refusing to separate them.

Canterbury afforded Bell the opportunity of planning his own contribution to English literature, although the work of writing was not begun until later. One argument for his going to Canterbury rather than, for example, to a major city parish like his old one at Leeds, had been that there might be the leisure to write the biography of his old chief, Davidson. This work was envisaged on a considerable scale, and the old Archbishop had carefully built up the materials for what was originally thought of as an autobiography. When he abandoned the hope of writing this he was emphatic in desiring Bell to be his biographer.

In fact it was only after he became a bishop, when Davidson had died, that Bell began to write the great Life. It appeared in two solid black volumes in 1935, garnished with erudite and often entertaining epigraphs at the top of each chapter, and copious in its quotations from Davidson's dictated memoranda and the letters he sent and received. It was somewhat bold to prepare the book on such a scale, long though the Archbishop's life had been, and fascinating as had been his contacts with the great and the prominent from the point when, early in his life, he had gone as a young chaplain to Lambeth. The fashion for the multi-volume biography had gone: Lytton Strachey had assassinated it with the narrow stiletto of *Eminent Victorians*. (It is a strange irony that it now appears to be returning, with Michael Holroyd's vast two-volume life of Strachey.) And if any man was an eminent Victorian Davidson was, at least in his earlier life.

Bell's Life was nevertheless a great success from the moment that it was published. It was far more than a fount of information on all important ecclesiastical issues for the long period during which its subject had been engaged in the central life of the church. For all its length it was remarkably free from longueurs. It was beautifully written, with both clarity and vividness. The organization of the book was excellent, and this was of particular importance because the range of concerns reflected in its pages was exceedingly wide.

For our concern with Bell himself the publication of his one great book has a double significance. It is in itself a major literary achievement, only occasioning the sad reflection that the inordinate pressures of a bishop's life, as they went on and grew, denied us anything more from his pen that approached this calibre. For a diocesan bishop to have written such a book in the interstices of leisure in an over-pressed life is a mark of Bell's rigorous discipline, as well as of his literary powers.

But the other significance is that the preparation and writing of the book gave him a command of all the significant developments of church life, at home and abroad, across more than half a century. Moreover, it reinforced the direct and personal influence of the Archbishop whom he had served across those ten years at Lambeth. Bell's *Davidson* was to be a constant point of reference for church historians in the years to come: but it was Davidson's Bell who was to take a noble share in making church history.

NOTES

1. and 2. Quoted in Jasper. p. 19.

3. F. R. Barry, *Mervyn Haigh*, SPCK 1964, pp. 110–111; but see also a curiously contrasted reaction in J. G. Lockhart, *Cosmo Gordon Lang*, Hodder & Stoughton 1949, pp. 316–317.

4. *Mervyn Haigh*, p. 98.

5. G. K. A. Bell, *Randall Davidson*, OUP 1935, Vol. ii, pp. 900–901 (afterwards quoted as *Davidson*).

6. *Davidson*, Vol. ii, p. 753.

7. *Davidson*, Vol. ii, pp. 756–770.

8. *Davidson*, Vol. ii, pp. 777–778.

9. *Davidson*, Vol. ii, p. 903.

10. Jasper, p. 30

11. R. C. Mackie, review of Jasper, *Scottish Journal of Theology*, Vol. 21, No. 1, March 1968, pp. 108–110.

12. *Cosmo Gordon Lang*, p. 313.

3 An Ecumenical Prophet in the Making

Four years before Bell joined Davidson the Archbishop had played a notable part in the most influential event in the Christian history of our century. He had spoken at the first public meeting of the World Missionary Conference, held at Edinburgh in 1910. That conference is usually regarded as marking the beginning of the modern ecumenical movement. It was not the first world missionary conference (one had been held at Liverpool in 1860), but it was the first to make a determined attempt to break out of the rather conservative evangelical ethos that had determined the character of earlier gatherings. It was also the first to take seriously the preparation in research and study that should precede such a widely representative gathering, and emphatically the first to issue in the creation of a permanent expression of the will of divided Christians to study and act together. The continuation committee of the Edinburgh conference developed into the International Missionary Council, the ecumenical movement's first organ.

Davidson did not lightly undertake to address so mixed an ecclesiastical gathering. Many months went by before he committed himself, but when he did the commitment was complete. He saw the significance of what had been begun in the Free Church assembly hall of his native Scotland, and he sought opportunity to involve his young chaplain, for whom he foresaw so influential a future, in the developing movement. He had confidence that Bell's remarkable shrewdness for one so young would enable him to avoid the dangers of excessive enthusiasm as the burgeoning of the ecumenical cause became exciting.

Bell, however, brought his own personal commitment to the cause of unity. He did not have to await Davidson's influence, and it may be asked whether Davidson, for all his vision, was not too hamstrung by prudence to make an adequate response to what was being born. Bell belonged to that generation whose ecumenical ardour was kindled by Tissington Tatlow and the Student Christian Movement, and which dared to bring young men of different denominations together in the very years which saw establishment and nonconformity locked in the bitter struggle that centred on education issues. While at Wells Bell had shared in a tent run at the student camp at Baslow (precurser of the famous Swanwick and, like that conference centre, in Derbyshire). Characteristically, when the Wells students thereafter arranged a weekly service of intercession for Christian unity it was Bell who drew up the litany for the purpose.[1] (The same deep concern that Christian unity should be sought by prayer and not only by work appeared when he was entrusted with his most influential ecumenical office in 1949. When he was chairman of the central committee of the World Council of Churches, and the first full meeting was held in his see city of Chichester, he made arrangements to enable the members of the committee regularly to pray for one another by name.)

There is strong evidence, too, of the degree to which Bell stirred the primate to ecumenical action, as well as of the latter giving his chaplain the opportunities of ecumenical experience. Canon Jasper has revealed that even before Bell joined the Lambeth staff he had pressed on the Archbishop the need for Christians of all denominations to face to-

41

gether the issues raised by the war, and that the one-day meeting in October 1914, attended by some fifty representatives of the Church of England, the major Free Churches and the Quakers, which Bell was authorized to arrange, was based on his own initiative.[2]

It is striking that this first, and very brief, ecumenical conference for which Bell was to take the initiative (when still only thirty-one) brought together so many of the strands which were to be there throughout his service of the movement for Christian unity. It was to be in what came to be called 'Life and Work' rather than in 'Faith and Order' that he gave his primary service (although late in his episcopate he told one of his younger clergy, Peter Bide, that if he had to begin again he would make the other choice). Life and Work, as we shall see, took its origin in the vision of the great Swedish archbishop, Nathan Söderblom of Uppsala. He was convinced that Christian churches were called upon not just to pursue the missionary cause with greatly increased co-operation, but unitedly to face the challenges which the twentieth century was throwing up with ever-increasing complexity. Nowhere did that challenge appear more sharply than in war, and it was during the second great world war of our era that Bell was to be called to a remarkable witness, and a rare place in that creation of a spiritual *Una Sancta* transcending the divisions of war which gave heart and courage to many persecuted and suffering Christians.

That single day's conference at Lambeth Palace in October 1914 prefigured Bell's ecumenical service. It was another day at the Palace which was to usher in his opportunity of serving on the world scene. On that day, 15 April 1921, Randall Davidson was to receive for an hour's talk in the course of a day weighted with much business that Swedish archbishop who passionately longed for the calling of a

Universal Christian Conference on Life and Work. In perhaps the most entertaining pages of his big biography Bell tells of the contest of wits between the two archbishops, the one cautious, prudential and weighty, the other enthusiastic, mercurial and vivacious.[3] Bell appears anonymously as 'the chaplain' who prepared a sheet of paper listing the matters on which the two archbishops might talk. Söderblom rewrote it, as he waited for Davidson, and renumbered it so that the proposed conference headed the list, only to be thwarted by Davidson's amused determination to reverse the order in the actual conversation. Bell, present only as chaplain during that conflict of priorities, was in large measure to succeed Söderblom as the chief protagonist of Life and Work issues in the ecumenical movement.

Söderblom had in fact already marked Bell as an important person. This was partly, though not exclusively, because of his relationship to Lambeth. In 1919 at Oud Wassenaar, near The Hague, a conference attended by some sixty participants had been held under the auspices of yet another of the pioneering ecumenical bodies, the World Alliance for Promoting International Friendship through the Churches. Bell was present at it, though not as a full delegate.[4] The gravest problem that it faced, again prefiguring much in Bell's experience in the later war, was the problem of war guilt and the willingness of the German delegates to acknowledge it. The most important item of business was the proposed Universal Christian Conference on Life and Work. The day after the discussion of this Söderblom wrote to his wife:

The Conference, the ecumenical, was dealt with yesterday. Now it will be taken over by us in the North. We have Bell with us, therefore, I presume, also Canterbury. Otherwise it will have to be with us, Germany, the British Free Churches, Holland, Switzerland, Hungary, America, without the Church of England. . . .[5]

Even Söderblom's enthusiasm, together with the dominant role some Anglicans, notably Bishop Talbot of Winchester, had played at Oud Wassenaar, failed to make him certain that Bell's presence denoted Davidson's full support. Bell was in fact only an observer, and later events (including the amusing interview two years later at Lambeth) only served to reveal Davidson's doubts. Like all archbishops of the Church of England in the twentieth century he had to be persuaded that the word 'ecumenical' was being given its true content, and was not being used as an unjustifiable synonym for 'pan-Protestant'. Certainly the Swiss representatives as firmly wished invitations to be restricted to Protestant churches as Davidson was emphatic that Roman Catholic and Orthodox participation should be clearly invited, whatever might be the response.[6]

Davidson's unwillingness to be committed led to no Anglican being present at the meeting convened at Paris two months later to carry the proposal further. The Archbishop felt that he had made the conditions for the co-operation of the Church of England quite clear, and a delegation was superfluous. Nevertheless, general approval was given to the proposal at the Paris meeting, and a far larger and more representative gathering was planned at Geneva the following year to carry the whole matter further. This Geneva meeting was limited to Protestant churches and therefore, since one of Davidson's clear conditions was ignored, no Anglican delegation attended.

Bell, however, was present for another conference in Geneva and was invited to attend some of the meetings.

Söderblom reported to Mrs Söderblom in his staccato manner about his contribution: 'Before [Bell] left yesterday morning, he managed to render invaluable service as secretary. On Monday and in the French–German question: gallant, a man of honour, capable.'[7]

Whatever conditions Davidson laid down, his chaplain became convinced that the proposed Universal Conference was a right step and, in the years that led up to the holding of the conference at Stockholm in 1925, Söderblom relied on Bishop Frank Theodore Woods (of Peterborough, later of Winchester) and Bell as Anglican lieutenants.[8] Bell's new duties at Canterbury prevented his sharing in the British forerunner of Stockholm, the Conference on Politics, Economics and Citizenship held the previous year in Birmingham. This gathering was dominated by William Temple, whose ecumenical comprehensiveness and dazzling brilliance were almost to obscure Bell's pioneering contribution until the two could be looked at from a longer perspective. COPEC, as the Birmingham conference came to be called, was only national in scope, but it was infinitely better devised than the international gathering at Stockholm. It had learned the lesson of 'Edinburgh 1910' in terms of careful preparation. Stockholm relied too much on the inspirational techniques of earlier ecumenical gatherings, and the intellectual range and effervescent enthusiasm of a Söderblom were no substitute for the almost ruthless intellectual discipline and strategic planning of J. H. Oldham, who had been secretary of Edinburgh and its preparation. When the second Life and Work conference came to be held at Oxford in 1937, Oldham was fulfilling his Edinburgh role, and the difference was immense.

But though Bell was not uncritical of some of the arrangements at Stockholm, it represented to him the fulfilment of a great vision. Writing almost thirty years later he said: 'Beyond doubt this Conference was a landmark in the history of the Christian Churches since the Reformation.' After a strong tribute to Söderblom as the moving spirit of the whole enterprise he wrote (surely referring principally to his old chief at Lambeth):

> No one who was not in touch with authoritative Church opinion at that time can at this distance easily understand how difficult it was to convince the leaders of the Churches of the need of coming together, for a purpose difficult to translate into very concrete terms, in this necessarily dramatic way.[9]

Bell in that sentence reveals how much he had become Söderblom's man as well as Davidson's man. The pragmatic caution of the latter was now in some degree offset by the visionary enthusiasm of the former. The shy young Dean of Canterbury had become convinced of the need for an element of the dramatic as well as the practical in the witness to Christian unity and the Christian message to a preoccupied world. It was a conviction that he was to retain to the end of his life.

'Stockholm' marked the emergence of Bell as an ecumenical leader in his own right. He was still only forty-three.* Bell was now no longer seen as another's chaplain, but as in the full sense a leader. He was a member of the group that prepared the message of the conference. He edited the volume of the proceedings of the conference that was published in English. That volume was to record some prophetic words he spoke to the conference himself on the last day of its meeting:

> We can say that we at least resolve, we six hundred, that we will strive for reconciliation and co-operation: that in times of doubt, across frontiers which divide, we shall remember one another as brethren, and as brothers, putting aside distrust and suspicion, seek to understand our brothers' deeds, our brothers' words.[10]

This was a resolve that Bell was to maintain and exemplify when fourteen years later Europe was again to be engulfed and divided by war.

More important for the future than Bell's public role as

---

* Stockholm marked the beginning of international ecumenical experience for one a great deal younger, who was to be Bell's close colleague in the succeeding years, Willem Adolf Visser 't Hooft, first general secretary of the World Council of Churches.

46

speaker, committee man and editor, were two elements in his Stockhom experience. One was that he confirmed and widened the friendships made at earlier international ecumenical meetings. Men like Eivind Berggrav of Norway, Adolf Deissmann of Germany, and Archbishop Germanos of Thyatira became personal friends, while Söderblom's regard for him, expressed strikingly three years earlier by his command to Albert Schweitzer not to pass through London without seeing Bell,[11] was strongly confirmed. The other element was that he had so commended himself to all that he was inevitably a member of the continuation committee set up as the conference at Stockholm closed. Henceforth his base in ecumenical work at the world level was secure. The continuation committee was less than Bell's own vision for the future, which was of an International Council on Life and Work,[12] but it was one of the chief elements that led to the formation of something far more representative and comprehensive, the World Council of Churches. In fact, by 1930 it had become transformed into the Universal Council of Bell's vision. A year later the chief progenitor of Life and Work, Söderblom of Uppsala, was dead. Henceforth Bell was no longer under the shadow of the two great archbishops whom in very different ways and relationship he had served. A long apprenticeship to these two varied men, each charged with immense responsibilities, had not stifled Bell's leadership. In his quiet, patient way he had amassed a great store of experience, and had made his own judgment on the contrasted emphases and methods of the cautious, wise, pragmatic Scot at Lambeth, and the vivid, visionary personality of the Swedish scholar who brought a new international fame to the see of Uppsala. The man who was to stand where he stood because, in Luther's words, 'he could do no other' during the second world war, was still Davidson's Bell; but he was also Söderblom's Bell. It was not for nothing that the last sermon of Bell's life was on the text which is placed on Söderblom's tomb in his cathedral.

Even before the archbishop's death his ill-health had forced some reduction of his burden of leadership. Bell quietly moved to the lead in Life and Work. Nils Ehrenström has written:

> With rare distinction and gentle firmness, the Bishop of Chichester (Bell) guided the Council as its chairman during some of its most critical years. His handling of the relations with the German Churches, in a time of fierce struggle which placed before the ecumenical movement perplexing and difficult choices, was a masterpiece of pastoral statecraft.[13]

The curate at Leeds and the don at Oxford had become via his service at Lambeth, and the quickening of his zeal for a Christian unity relevant to this century's problems by Nathan Söderblom, a Christian leader of international stature.

Since 1929 he had been the Bishop of Chichester. His see was an ancient one and, partly by reason of the awkward situation of his cathedral and home in relation to the diocese, a particularly demanding one. Bell worked hard as a diocesan bishop, as he worked hard at everything that he undertook, but he was clear that the office of bishop was never purely local. He was a bishop of the whole Church of God, and the fact that he had become a diocesan bishop while still in his mid-forties meant that he had the energy to discharge local and wider responsibilities with vigour. The passage of the years in no way diminished the industry, and if the energy was in any degree abated it was abundantly compensated for by experience.

Bell certainly believed that a bishop rightly committed himself to extra-diocesan tasks, but in no way did he regard his see as merely giving him a standing for world-wide service. The Bishop of Bristol, Dr Oliver Tomkins, recalls during his own service of the World Council of Churches as a staff member calling at Chichester to discuss some Council business. He found Bell writing by hand a letter to one of his clergy whose wife had died.

> Later in the day, in answer to some request of mine to demand his time for the WCC, he said, 'After all, I *have* got a diocese!' I always felt that this closeness to local church life on the part of its leaders is one advantage which episcopal churches have in ecumenical affairs, and certainly G.K.A.B. was always measuring ecumenical actions and words by their relevance to Sussex or their credibility there. The Sussex Council of Churches was created to that end.*

That strange phrase used by Nils Ehrenström to describe Bell's chairmanship of the Universal Christian Council for Life and Work, 'a masterpiece of pastoral statecraft', is in its unusual way an accurate summary. He had become a statesman of the World Church, but he was, and remained, a pastoral statesman.

* See chapter 6, pp. 106–108.

NOTES

1. Jasper, p. 11.
2. Jasper, p. 23.
3. *Davidson*, Vol. ii, pp. 1048–1051.
4. Jasper, pp. 57–58, states that Bell went as a member of the Anglican delegation, but Söderblom's biographer says that Bell's name was not included on the list of delegates.
5. Bengt Sundkler, *Nathan Söderblom*, Lutterworth Press 1968, p. 232.
6. Nils Karlström, 'Movements for International Friendship and Life and Work, 1910–1925', *A History of the Ecumenical Movement 1517–1948* ed. Ruth Rouse and Stephen Neill, SPCK 1954, p. 535 (later referred to as 'Rouse-Neill').
7. Sundkler, p. 240.
8. Sundkler, p. 351.
9. G. K. A. Bell, *The Kingship of Christ*. Penguin Books 1954, pp. 26–27.
10. *The Stockholm Conference*, ed G. K. A. Bell, OUP 1936, pp. 680–681.
11. Jasper, p. 31.
12. Nils Ehrenström, 'Movements for International Friendship and Life and Work, 1925–1948', Rouse-Neill, p. 552.
13. Rouse-Neill, p. 555.

4   The Crisis in the German Church

30th January 1933 was a day fraught with appalling consequences for all who were to live through the next decade and beyond. On that day Adolf Hitler came to power in Germany, and democracy died. For George Bell what happened in Germany on that day directly determined the character of the rest of his life. Had he not become caught up in the German church struggle, and consequently with the German resistance movement during the war, he would have been a peripheral figure in the Christian story of our century, admired as a gifted biographer and as an Anglican ecumenical pioneer but scarcely warranting inclusion in such a series as that in which this volume appears.

One whose primary duty was to be father-in-God to one of the more affluent and conservative dioceses of the Church of England seems a strange figure to be so constantly and intimately caught up in the affairs of a country whose language, despite a resolute attempt to learn it during his time as Dean of Canterbury, defeated him to the end of his life.[1] (In this, as in so much else, Bell was deeply English: his wide culture did not include the gift of modern languages.) Little in his upbringing or experience seemed obviously to equip him to play the part that he did as the invincible protagonist of that 'Confessing' Church which came into being to withstand Hitler's pressures upon the German Evangelical Church.

There were, nevertheless, three elements in his experience that fitted him to assume leadership when the challenge came. One was the office that he held. He was the key figure in the Life and Work movement. Until the close of the meeting of the Universal Christian Council for Life and Work in 1934 he was the chairman. Thereafter he remained one of the presidents and, more important, chairman of the administrative committee. This gave him a definite position which he did not hesitate to use to intervene when crucial issues were at stake in Germany.

Again, as we have seen, he was in many things the spiritual heir of Söderblom. He had none of Söderblom's deep Europeanism (Söderblom had served as chaplain in Calais and Paris and as professor in Leipzig, as well as having a ready command of the major European languages and a profound knowledge of the main movements of European thought.) But Bell was a man of 'Stockholm'. The message of that conference, in drafting which Bell had had a major share, included these words:

> We have also set forth the guiding principles of a Christian inter-nationalism, equally opposed to a national bigotry and a weak cosmopolitanism. We have affirmed the universal character of the Church, and its duty to preach and practise the love of the brethren. We have considered the relation of the individual conscience to the state.[2]

Developments in Nazi Germany were to contradict that Stockholm vision at every point, by exalting nationalism in its most paranoic form, denying the universal character of the church, and seeking to obliterate the rights of individual conscience by assertion of the absolute claim of the state. Bell was equipped to discern with total clarity from the very first the real nature of what was going on in Germany.

Moreover, although at first sight the obduracy and remorseless pertinacity with which he pursued his course of public criticism of the Nazi regime seemed a strange development in one who was not only Söderblom's heir but much more patently Davidson's, the discontinuity was more apparent than real. It was not only that a stream of letters to *The Times* and a succession of informal groups gathering at the Athenaeum marked the progress of Bell's concern, and thus he used the instruments of that 'establishment' in which Davidson had moved with such ease. It was that Davidson's former chaplain followed his old chief in being deeply concerned in the major political struggle of his time. In Davidson's time, apart from issues raised by the first world war (to which reference has already been made), it was questions like home rule for Ireland, and the House of Lords struggle which engaged the Archbishop's close concern. Bell's prophetic genius saw that what was going on in Germany was *the* issue in the 1930s, and despite the constant demands of his own day-to-day work in his diocese he gave much of the best of his mind and energy to this concern. He early discerned what Ehrenström was to describe as 'an historical situation in which the perennial conflict between the Church and the world was again reaching a new pitch of terrible intensity, due to the on-slaught of militant secular and neo-pagan forces'.[3]

Bell wrote some years after the second world war ended:

A new impetus, however, was given to the ecumenical movement by the rise of the National Socialist State in Germany in 1933. It was the Life and Work side which was most strongly affected.[4]

The first of those two sentences is far more remarkable than superficially may appear. That it served as an impetus was due to a few men of whom Bell was the chief. It could have served as the destruction of the infant ecumenical movement. Within less than ten years after the Stockholm gathering, which was the first major non-missionary ecumenical world conference, the movement's responsible leadership faced the question of which church was in fact the true Christian church in one of the major European countries.

The Faith and Order side of the ecumenical movement had held its first world conference at Lausanne in 1927. By its very nature it was more deeply ecclesiastical in character and, handling as it did the most fissile material in regard to church divisions, was bound to be almost pedantically circumspect in sticking to the rules. (Dietrich Bonhoeffer was to discover this in correspondence with Dr Leonard Hodgson, the secretary of Faith and Order, in 1935.)[5] But Life and Work, if less firmly ecclesiastical, was still precarious in its condition, and the world economic crisis had at one point rendered even its survival doubtful. In Britain, unlike the World Alliance for Promoting International Friendship through the Churches (which had gained the influential support of men like Sir Stafford Cripps), there was little organized support for the Life and Work movement. At one major meeting of the Universal Christian Council Bell was the sole representative from England.

It would have been excusable, and even natural, if a movement still seeking a broad base of support in the churches, and its own way forward, had been very cautious in handling the issues raised by the German church struggle. After all, it was the initial and never wholly stifled criticism of every ecumenical initiative from the Edinburgh conference in 1910 onwards that organs would be created which would unwarrantably interfere with the life of individual churches. If the Universal Christian Council started taking sides in the internal affairs of the German church would not such suspicions have been proved to be totally justified?

From the vantage point of almost forty years after the

beginning of that struggle in Germany it is easy to see that had the Life and Work movement tried to push this issue away to the circumference it would have forfeited any claim to relevance to the central issue of that time. It can have been far from as clear to many then. The glory of Bell's contribution to the whole development of Life and Work is found in his determination that what was happening in Germany should be seen as the central issue. The eventual examination of the whole wide question of totalitarianism as the major theme of the second world conference of Life and Work, that on 'Church, Community and State' at Oxford in 1937, owed far more to J. H. Oldham than to Bell, and a biographer must beware of a natural tendency to exaggerate the contribution of his subject to the movement. To Oldham rather than to Bell must be attributed much of the achievement of that Oxford conference which had been prepared for with the intellectual rigour which the Stockholm gathering had lacked. One knowledgable and astringent critic has judged that had it been left to Bell the Life and Work movement would never have moved out of mediocrity. It was Oldham who made certain that mediocrity was not a word that anyone would be likely to apply to the second world conference of the movement.

Bell's particular achievement at the point was different and two-fold. He ensured that there was a living movement which could mount so essential a conferring of Christian leaders as they stood almost on the threshold of another world war. He also determined that the theme of that gathering should be what it was. Naturally, others shared with him in this achievement but, because of the position which he held, any faltering or equivocation on his part would almost certainly have left the movement in the shallows. When in 1954 Bell wrote those words about a new impetus being given to the ecumenical movement by the rise of

Nazism he was pointing to the actual result. It could have been far otherwise. His own humility masked the alternative effect that the rise of Hitler to power could have had upon the still fragile organs of ecumenical co-operation.

Strangely, Bell was in Berlin when Hitler came to power and celebrated his fiftieth birthday five days later amidst a great sea of flags being flown to celebrate the Nazi victory. The meetings of the executive committee of the World Alliance, the Geneva secretaries, and the executive of Life and Work were held in succession in the German capital across the very days on which Hitler was assuming supreme control over the Reich. It was a curiously fitting prelude to years in which Bell was to find his peace of mind constantly invaded by the German question; and years, too, in which his prophetic role in regard to the Confessing Church and its opposition to Hitler was to lead to grave misunderstanding and hostility towards him.

Within less than a month after his accession to power Hitler, using the occasion of the Reichstag fire, promulgated a decree that was to abolish almost all constitutional rights of the individual until Hitler himself was no more. Eberhard Bethge remarks that it made possible the concentration camps. It was the basis of totally arbitrary rule.

There followed the actions which were to mark the pathological recession into barbarism which Nazism proved to be – boycott and persecution of all Jews, exaltation of Nordic blood (and the consequent hounding of all with some admixture of 'non-Aryan' race), and the full apparatus of totalitarianism. This included the attempt to create a national church which would be Hitler's creature, headed by Ludwig Müller, a former army chaplain wholly lacking in any distinction, but enjoying the dubious privilege of Hitler's confidence.

There were other acts of the new government which

seemed to promise much good for the nation. It had been weakly governed, and not only shared the world-wide economic depression with its consequence in mass unemployment, but still smarted under a sense of defeat and disgrace. Hitler appeared to many inside the Christian church as the saviour of a nation threatened by godless Bolshevism and eroded in its confidence by bad government, international Jewish finance and the will of its former enemies to keep it in subjection. One of Bonhoeffer's biographers quotes the utterance of one of the Evangelical Church's general superintendents at the time of Hitler's first moves against the Jews:

> To me it is fairly understandable, because of what Jewry by its control of the Press, finance, the theatre, etc., has done to us . . . that justifiable collective anger, even when the people's frame of mind is not specifically anti-Semitic, should for once vent itself in violence. Never for a second has the black, red and gold flag [i.e. of the Weimar Republic] had any place either in my heart or in my home. I have always been a man of the extreme right.[6]

With some men of that type in the leadership of the church we need not be surprised that when 'German Christians' (a group avowedly committed to total support of Hitler), pressed for the adoption of the notorious Aryan clause within the church in Prussia they were successful. That clause, introduced to exclude from the civil service all of Jewish or partly Jewish descent, could now be used to extrude all Christian ministers having any Jewish blood at all. It was in opposition to this that Dietrich Bonhoeffer first took his stand.

The gradual emergence of a body of Christians who, from different standpoints and in varying degrees, fought the attempts of Hitler to impose his will upon the church, and fought, too, a spirit of subservience within the church, is the story of the creation of what came to be a church within the church – the Confessing Church,* as it came to be known.

On 4 September 1933, the gathering which came to be called the 'Brown Synod' of the church in Prussia was held. The nickname was due to the number of participants wearing the brown shirts of Nazi party members, and the synod replaced the ten general superintendents by ten 'German Christian' bishops, thus purging from the administration of the church all who were not sympathetic to the new regime. Some, including Martin Niemöller, pressed for the creation of a wholly free church.

This idea was not supported, but instead there was born the first organ of the Confessing Church, which was to fight for its freedom without creating a schism; this was the *Pfarrernotbund*, the Emergency League of Pastors. In its first form it was pledged to four points:

1 To renew allegiance to the Scriptures and the Creed.
2 To resist any attack upon them.
3 To give material and financial help to those who suffered through oppressive laws of violence.
4 To repudiate the Aryan paragraph.[7]

The Confessing Church was to have other organs, including the secret seminary for the training of pastors at Finkenwalde, of which Bonhoeffer was the head.

The line between the official church and the Confessing Church was not always easy to draw. Not all in the official church were of one mind, and certainly not all in the Confessing Church were. Moreover, the Confessing Church was not in schism; there had been no disruption such as came in Scotland in 1843. But just as the Free Church of Scotland, which 'came out at the Disruption', claimed to be no new church but the true Church of Scotland, so this Confessing Church, even while not separating, claimed to be the true German Evangelical Church. Bonhoeffer during the follow-

* Bell and his official biographer always call it the Confessional Church, but this is an unusual usage.

ing year wrote in this uncompromising vein to H. L. Henriod, the general secretary both of the World Alliance and of Life and Work:

> There is not the claim or even the wish to be a Free Church besides the *Reichskirche*, but there is the claim to be the only theologically and legally legitimate Evangelical Church in Germany, and accordingly you cannot expect this church to set up a new constitution, since it is based on the very constitution which the *Reichskirche* has neglected.[8]

It was in the adjudication of that claim that Bell found himself so deeply engaged on so many fronts. Who could fitly represent the evangelical Christians of Germany at such a time in ecumenical conference with their brethren of other lands? Making a judgment upon this inevitably involved making a judgment upon what was going on in Germany, both in regard to the actions of the secular power and the reaction of the church to those actions. Such a judgment must rest upon as accurate information as could be secured, and this by definition was not easy to obtain when a totalitarian state had taken control of all means of communication. More than this, the information that was secured needed evaluation.

It was at this point that Bell secured the inestimable help of one who has been judged to be one of the most influential Christians of our time, Dietrich Bonhoeffer, the outstanding young German theologian who was hanged on Hitler's personal orders at the age of thirty-nine. His *Letters and Papers from Prison*[9] has been perhaps the most seminal Christian book of the third quarter of our century. From the moment of his first meeting with Bell until he was executed in the spring woods at Flossenbürg on 9 April 1945, Bonhoeffer's life was entwined with that of the English bishop he came to speak of as 'Uncle George'. They shared a common birthday, but Bell was twenty-three years older.

Bonhoeffer's most intimate friend and biographer, Eberhard Bethge, says of him that 'the only personalities to whom he granted real authority over him were Karl Barth and Dr Bell, the Bishop of Chichester'.[10] It was to George Bell of Chichester that Bonhoeffer sent the last message of his life as he was led away to the place of execution.

That tragic moment, however, was twelve years away when Bell first came to know and appreciate the young German pastor. They had already met at Geneva, but the opportunity for a close relationship came when Bonhoeffer deliberately chose to leave his teaching position in Berlin to be pastor of two small German congregations in London, living in Forest Hill near the church of one of them. That choice had been made when Bonhoeffer saw the need to interpret in Britain the true meaning of what was going on in Germany, and within the Evangelical Church there. Within three weeks of his arrival he was invited to the palace at Chichester.

Mary Bosanquet has written:

> Bonhoeffer soon gained a filial affection for this great-hearted statesman of the Church, and Bell for his part valued the integrity and acuteness of mind of this passionate young German, who saw the struggle as a struggle for the purity of the Christian faith itself, transcending national boundaries. With the humility of a great man, Bell allowed himself to be informed and even instructed, gaining an insight into the issues involved which was second to that of no other man outside Germany.[11]

On the basis of this knowledge Bell took the lead in informing influential British opinion, largely through a constant stream of letters to *The Times*. He was also equipped to handle the question when it inevitably came before the international Christian forum which Life and Work represented. The executive committee of the movement met at Novi Sad in Yugoslavia in September 1933. The representatives of the German Evangelical Church were led by Theodor

Heckel, head of the Ecclesiastical Foreign Ministry. Bishop Heckel, as he became, was a man of wholly different calibre from Müller. The latter was a man of no culture, holding office merely because of his complaisance towards the regime. Heckel was able and a genuinely committed Christian and churchman, who was able to put a sympathetic interpretation on the coming of Hitler to power because of the disorder that had preceded that event. As Theodore Gill puts it, perhaps a little rhetorically, for Bonhoeffer Heckel 'chose wrong, and so he was the respected enemy, resisted but not hated, double damned in a hell of tragic ambiguities'.[12] Only when Heckel's true stature is appreciated can the full measure of Bell's difficulties be assessed.

Heckel was naturally anxious to interpret the events of the past months, since the advent of Hitler to power, in the most favourable light. The minutes of the meeting read:

[Heckel] painted a clear picture of the vast changes and preliminary reconstruction in Nation, State and Church, and sought to clarify the great questions and tasks which hereby assume particular importance for the whole work of the churches in the ecumenical field.[13]

(Connoisseurs of the ecumenical art of handling the unpalatable without direct offence can treasure this splendid example of the genre.) In the course of the speech, the central contents of which were to be so neutrally recorded, Heckel had in fact scoffed at all the ideals for which the Stockholm conference had stood. 'Its message is obsolete,' he said, '. . . the off-spring of the humanitarian ideals of the Enlightenment and the French Revolution. . . . The rising Reformation theology today would put a critical question-mark at almost every sentence in it.'[14]

This was taking the battle into the enemy camp with a vengeance. It suggested that the authors of the Stockholm message, and not the ecclesiastical supporters of Nazism, were unconscious traitors to the faith. One of the authors,

Wilfred Monod of France, responded by expressing his regret that the German churchman had failed to mention in his account what had recently happened in his country, for the meeting at Novi Sad had begun only five days after the 'Brown Synod' which had installed the 'German Christian' bishops in Prussia. There was no mention in Heckel's speech of the imposition of the Aryan clause on the Christian Church. Monod believed that a Christian assembly would have been interested to hear of these things.

Another author of the Stockholm message, Bell, was in the chair. Bell resolved on bringing forward a resolution which could only result in the recorded disagreement of the leaders of the German delegation. This may seem a small and inevitable result of taking the only stand which Christian men with any integrity could take, but it marked a departure from all previous ecumenical practice. Bell had sought to reduce the openness of the split as much as possible over a tense week-end, but his statemanship in trying to avoid a break-up of Life and Work was never used to obscure the true situation in Germany. The resolution which he brought forward included these words:

> ... grave anxieties were expressed by the representatives of different churches in Europe and America in particular with regard to the severe action taken against persons of Jewish origin, and the serious restrictions placed upon freedom of thought and expression in Germany. ...

In one sense this was only factual. Such anxieties had been expressed. But the decision to state it by resolution was of real significance.

Of equal importance was the invitation to Bell to write on behalf of the committee to the German church government. This was a far more public act. It henceforth identified Bell in the most emphatic manner as a critic of what was happening to the Christian cause in Germany. The letter was addressed to Reichbishop Müller. Written on 23 October, it was issued to the press some days later. It contained a quotation from a declaration made by no fewer than two thousand pastors to the National Synod at Wittenberg which had been held between the Novi Sad meeting and the writing of the letter. The declaration made with this massive support showed that the deep concern felt by Christians elsewhere in the world, on behalf of whom Bell wrote, was not an anxiety on behalf of some minor eccentric group. The quotation read:

> In critical and important meetings of the Synod the present majority of its members have refused the minority its fundamental right of giving advice and of free speech, even in regard to questions which touch upon the essential nature of the Church and its commission. Church life has been kept by force for several months under coercive control of a single group in the Church. It ought not to be, that in denial of brotherly love the Church of Jesus Christ should, through the domination of force, be made a kingdom of this world.[15]

Müller sought to be reassuring, but his reply was contradicted by the swift movement of events in the church in Germany. In the following year Bell addressed an Ascension Day message to the churches, in his capacity as president of Life and Work. This action was taken on the strong advice of Bonhoeffer, who believed that the common cause of European Christianity was at stake. He pleaded with his older friend, 'Please do not remain silent now!'[16] Bonhoeffer was more than the initiator; he was responsible for a great deal of the contents of the letter, for Bell, with a remarkable humility in an acknowledged world leader in this field, had submitted his first draft to the German pastor who was still in his twenties. (We may note how well he had learned the lesson of Davidson's trust of a young man.)

There were two main purposes in this letter. One was to warn the churches so that there would be caution and judgment in resisting the wooing approaches of the German church government. Those approaches had already been disturbingly successful in regard to the Bishop of Gloucester, A. C. Headlam, a central figure in Faith and Order and in the foreign relations of the Church of England. The other purpose was to make clear that the German church question must inevitably occupy the centre of the stage in the forthcoming meeting of the full Universal Christian Council of Life and Work. This was due to be held at Fanö, in Denmark, in August. The letter ran:

I have been urged from many quarters to issue some statement to my fellow members of the Universal Christian Council for Life and Work upon the present position in the German Evangelical Church, especially as it affects the other Churches represented on the Universal Christian Council for Life and Work.

The situation is, beyond doubt, full of anxiety. To estimate it aright, we have to remember the fact that a revolution has taken place in the German State, and that as a necessary result the German Evangelical Church was bound to be faced with new tasks and many new problems requiring time for their full solution. It is nonetheless true that the present position is being watched by members of the Christian Churches abroad not only with great interest, but with a deepening concern. The chief cause of anxiety is the assumption by the Reichbishop in the name of the principle of leadership of autocratic powers unqualified by constitutional or traditional restraints which are without precedent in the history of the Church. The exercise of these autocratic powers by the Church government appears incompatible with the Christian principle of seeking in brotherly fellowship to receive the guidance of the Holy Spirit. It has had disastrous effects on the internal unity of the Church; and the disciplinary measures which have been taken by the Church government against Ministers of the Gospel on account of their loyalty to the fundamental principles of Christian truth have made a painful impression on Christian opinion abroad, already disturbed by the introduction of racial distinctions in the universal fellowship of the Christian Church. No wonder that voices should be raised in Germany itself making a solemn pronouncement before the whole Christian world on the dangers to which the spiritual life of the Evangelical Church is exposed.

There are indeed other problems which the German Evangelical Church is facing, which are the common concern of the whole of Christendom. These are such fundamental questions as those respecting the nature of the Church, its witness, its freedom and its relation to the secular power. At the end of August the Universal Council will be meeting in Denmark. The Agenda of the Council will inevitably include a consideration of the religious issues raised by the present situation in the German Evangelical Church. It will also have to consider the wider questions which affect the life of all the Churches in Christendom. . . .[17]

Even this forthright and widely circulated statement did not satisfy all Bonhoeffer's desires, which ran to the giving of an 'ultimatum' to Müller (the precise content of which it is not easy to discern): but he was deeply grateful for it and in expressing his thanks to Bell called it 'a living document of ecumenic and mutual responsibility'.[18] Recognition from the other side came later in the year when von Ribbentrop, then Hitler's special envoy, made a visit to Chichester itself to see Bell. Bell's was a voice that was marring the Hitler regime's attempt to give itself an attractive image beyond Germany.

But the attention which Bell and others were directing to the true nature of the situation in Germany did not avail in any way to lessen the progress towards a total and repulsive tyranny in which, at great personal risks, a noble company of Christians were bearing their witness. By the time the Fanö meeting came in August 1934, the tension was great. It included an event which so impressed itself on Bell that he referred to it twenty years later, even within the few lines he could spare for the meeting in his short volume on the World Council of Churches.

There was an extraordinary scene when a Nazi courier came by air from quarters attached to the new government in Germany, with instructions to the German Church delegates. The whole atmosphere of this meeting was tense, as there were anti-Nazi Germans secretly present as well as official delegates of the Evangelical Church.[19]

The official history of the ecumenical movement refers to the meeting of the Universal Christian Council at Fanö as 'perhaps the most critical and decisive meeting in its history'. It was this because, 'Here the Council solemnly resolved to throw its weight on the side of the Confessing Church in Germany against the so-called "German Christians" and by implication against the Nazi regime'.[20]

Bell faced the severest possible test of his ecumenical and international statesmanship in the preparation for the meeting and in the meeting itself. He was clear that any premature ostracism of the official church would only have the effect of closing doors that were still partly open. He was as clear that there must be representatives of the Confessing Church present. He was prepared, despite protests from the official German representatives, to use his powers as president to invite Bonhoeffer, and Dr Koch, President of the Westphalian Church and a senior leader of the Confessing Church, to be present. Koch in the end decided that it would be prudent not to attend. Bell was aware of the tight-rope that he walked in this matter. The whole basis of the ecumenical movement was, and is, that churches should themselves choose those who were to represent them. Abuse of his presidential powers would lay him open to the gravest criticism. But the situation was without precedent. A large part of the German church, and that which most disinterested outside observers judged to be most true to the gospel, was being excluded from any share in the official life of the church.

Bonhoeffer in fact attended. The meeting was stormy, with leaks to the press, demands from the German delegates that all discussions should be held in camera, and a grotesque statement by the air-borne envoy, Birnbaum, within a twenty-minute time-limit firmly maintained by Bell. Marc Boegner, present for the first time at the Universal Christian Council (but later to become the doyen of the French-speaking ecumenists) wrote in a letter from Fanö that it was 'the most incredible address you could imagine'.

C

There was not a single reference to what we find so heartbreaking in life today and particularly in the government of the Church. There were platitudes about the spiritual revival, the increase in the number of marriages and baptisms, the development of Christianity in the proletariat as a result of the National-Socialist revolution. . . . We just sat and gaped.[21]

Bell's tight-rope walk commended itself to the Universal Christian Council. He had used the right of the president to invite guests: the Council used its right under the rules to co-opt Dr Koch and Bonhoeffer to full membership. This action itself was the clearest declaration of where the Council stood, but it was further spelt out by resolution.

The Council desires to assure its brethren in the Confessional Synod of the German Evangelical Church of its prayers and heart-felt sympathy in their witness to the principles of the gospel, and of its resolve to maintain close fellowship with them.[22]

Bishop Heckel, on behalf of the official German delegation, protested at this and other declarations of the Council, saying 'The Delegation find in this an attitude to the internal situation of the German Church which transgresses the limits of the task of the Universal Christian Council in a very questionable way.'[23] More important, he managed to get a small clause inserted in the resolution supporting the Confessing Church. It stated that the Council 'wished to remain in friendly contact with all groups in the German Evangelical Church'.

It is hard to see how Bell, aware as he was of the danger of cutting off the non-Confessing side of the church from the possible influence of ecumenical contacts, could have objected to this. Bethge, however, in his biography of Bonhoeffer, regards this as allowing 'the Reich Church to put its foot inside the door'. He says that Bonhoeffer felt that Fanö represented 'an incomparable step forward for Christendom': only later was it realized that 'at Fanö the ecumenical movement had gone as far as it was ever to go in its commitment towards the Confessing Church'.[24]

But even Bethge has to admit that Bonhoeffer, too, did not take exception to the admitting of Heckel's clause. It is understandable that one like Bethge who lived and suffered for the Confessing cause should show impatience with anything but total recognition that that 'church within a church' represented the only true manifestation of the gospel. The fact remains that under Bell's eirenic but completely firm leadership the Universal Christian Council neither took refuge in platitudes nor closed the door to all fellowship with the officially appointed representatives of one of its largest member churches. Even reading Bethge's words, published in English some three years after Bell's official biography, it is impossible to quarrel with Canon Jasper's judicious verdict:

> Fanö, marking the end of Bell's period as chairman of the Council, was something of a personal triumph for him. The wisdom and courage evinced by the Council were largely the fruits of his own efforts – his gentle but steady control of the sessions and his ceaseless activity in the informal discussions.[25]

A more personal reaction to Bell's personality is given by Marc Boegner, writing in old age more than thirty years after the Fanö meeting.

> The chairman was George Bell, Bishop of Chichester, of whom I had had no more than a glimpse until that time; and it was a great joy to be able to learn to know him, to live in the light of his serenity, to see those intensely blue eyes of his fix themselves on one, as one walked up to him. To love him was indeed a blessing from heaven. The friendship he showed me during those crowded days on Fanö was the richest memory I brought back from France, and I still nurse it intact in my heart.[26]

It was perhaps due more than anything else to the spiritual quality of this man that while there had been deep tension, and there had been drama at Fanö, there had not been any

67

explosion. The stand of the Confessing Church had been supported, but the possibility of a more courageous stand on the part of the German church government had not been excluded. Before the year ended it even appeared as if the spirit of Fanö had triumphed, when Müller was forced to reinstate two bishops whom he had deposed. But from today's vantage-point we are compelled to realize that the Nazi regime would, and could, tolerate no show of independence at any point. The true church would have to go underground and suffer, for National Socialism could allow no element of freedom within the Reich.

There was much to discourage, but one of Bell's strongest characteristics was his steady refusal to be daunted by discouragement. He was like John Bunyan's pilgrim in this, no giant could him fright. We may feel today that there was no real hope that Hitler could be made to alter; Bell himself must often have despaired, but he felt compelled even as the darkness grew to 'work while it is day'. Members of the Universal Christian Council were urged to make constant representations to the ambassadors in their countries. The Archbishop of Canterbury, Lang (who was more open to Bell's urging than might have been expected) was pressed to make similar representations. Bell conferred with von Ribbentrop at the Athenaeum, and wrote to him more than once.

At one time it appeared that adjustments towards greater freedom were being made in the German church situation, and Dr Koechlin, the Swiss church leader with whom Bell was in correspondence for many years, felt that this was due to the pressure of British Christians, chiefly Bell. Bell met Hitler's deputy, Rudolf Hess, in 1935 informally at Hess's home in Berlin. He took the opportunity to press home on the Deputy Führer the need for the church to have a genuinely independent place in the life of the nation. Tactfully

68

he stressed the importance of the German church interna-
tionally.

> . . . I said that the Churches of the world had a great battle to
> fight against the things which were hostile to Christianity, and they
> wanted the full strength of the German Evangelical Church in this
> common fight. This was a very important point as it turned out.
> Frau Hess, who had been somewhat critical before I said this, said,
> 'Oh, that is why foreign Churches are interested in our Church
> conflict'; and she and Hess fully agreed that it was the business of
> the Churches to unite their forces against anti-God and anti-
> Christianity.[27]

(We may catch in the Hess response a glimpse of the
'bulwark against atheistic Communism' conviction which
was to send him some years later on his perverse and futile
one-man mission to Britain.) Bell's conversation was in
fact interrupted by the arrival of Hitler himself, but he and
the Hesses did not part without expressed determination
to keep in touch. Bell, indefatigable correspondent that he
was, did not fail to seize the opening, but the response of
Hess dwindled eventually into mere acknowledgment.

The church struggle continued, with weakening divisions
within the Confessing Church, and the determination of
men like Niemöller to refuse co-operation with the official
church, now headed by Wilhelm Zoellner, a hitherto neutral
and now retired Lutheran general superintendent.

Before the Universal Christian Council met at Chamby,
near Montreux, in August 1936 for the last meeting before
the world conference of Life and Work (due to be held
during the following year at Oxford on 'Church, Community
and State') the question of German church representation
had become wildly tangled. Zoellner's official group were
unwilling to attend if recognition were given to the Confessing Church. There could be no question of Koch and Bonhoeffer, duly co-opted at Fanö, being excluded. On the other
hand Bonhoeffer felt that it was 'no longer admissible that

69

the leading personalities of the Confessing Church should be treated as private individuals. The ecumenical movement should be asked whether it intended to recognize the Confessing Church as the only lawful church.'[28] In the event Koch and Bonhoeffer were there, with Otto Dibelius (post-war bishop of Berlin-Brandenburg) and Dr Böhm from the Confessing Church as visitors invited by Bell; and Zoellner headed the official group.

Bell showed his usual mixture of skill and determination before the event, and his almost inordinate capacity for work in the interstices of the meeting itself. The main result of this was a fragile agreement won between the German groups to aim at the election of a national church synod in which only the truly committed church members should vote.

This was a gallant attempt, and shows Bell in his role of tireless reconciler; but the situation was in fact growing more and more dark. Chamby had been a preparation for the Oxford conference, and one of the urgent issues regarding Germany was who would represent the church there at a world conference whose very theme was the relation between the church and the state. In the event there was no one there from either the official church or the Confessing Church, but only a couple of representatives of the tiny free churches who played a perhaps understandably pusillanimous and craven role. Martin Niemöller was by this time in prison, an imprisonment that was only to end when the second world war itself came to a close.

Meanwhile Bell was fighting within his own church against those who resented and resisted what they would have described as his mistaken obsession with the German church struggle. Chief amongst his opponents was the doughty Arthur Cayley Headlam, Bishop of Gloucester. (Such fierce argument went on at one student conference committee concerning which protagonist should be invited that the chairman banged on the table, and said, 'Which is it to be, Hell or Bedlam?') Headlam was a scholar of international repute, a leading figure in Faith and Order and Chairman of the Church of England Council for Foreign Relations. This Council was the arena in which some sharp conflicts were fought out between the two.

Headlam represented the right-wing fear of Bolshevism all too readily entertained by men of substance. He was a wealthy man, and his political judgments were controlled, probably unconsciously, by economic self-interest. He was all too ready to act as apologist for the Nazi line in the church struggle. When the formation of the Council for Foreign Relations was first proposed it was Headlam's own idea that Bell, then Dean of Canterbury, should be the effective chairman (actually vice-chairman, under the nominal chairmanship of the Archbishop of Canterbury). By the time the Council was formed Headlam seemed the obvious chairman, but the extent of his knowledge of the European churches, both Orthodox and Protestant, was no compensation for an almost wilful refusal to see what was increasingly obvious to all observers of the German scene. His personal integrity must acquit him of all malign intention; but the same could also be said of not a few in the 'Cliveden Set' and of Geoffrey Dawson whose use of *The Times* to dull the awareness of the governing classes of Britain to the true nature of the Nazi regime has earned the just condemnation even of that journal's official historian. Malign intention was not needed when fear of loss of wealth and privilege made men morally blind. It is the glory of George Bell's witness that he worked month by month to open men's eyes to reality. He received from not a few the kind of reaction that men make when they are forced to face the unpalatable. In some circles he was regarded rather like Churchill in those days, as a scaremonger and a man who had lost all sense of proportion. It is nevertheless to the credit of the bishops of the Church of England, and a measure of his achievement, that when Headlam moved the 'previous question' (i.e. that the resolution be not put) on a resolution by Bell in the Upper House of the Convocation of Canterbury, expressing concern over the sufferings of Christians in Germany, Headlam failed to find a seconder.[29]

Bell had achieved much in alerting Christian opinion to the nature of the church conflict in Germany, but the grotesquely evil character of the regime there meant that there could be no real chance that it could be influenced by world Christian opinion. There might be apparent yielding on this or that point, but such responses were purely tactical. The relentless purpose of Hitler and his gang to subjugate all the forces of freedom and independence within the Reich went on unimpeded save for a passing moment.

When the Oxford conference met, Bell was the prime mover in the preparation of a special message to the German church. The fears of the representatives of the German free churches led to great difficulties in the handling of this message, but the effect of it at the receiving end was as heartening as Bell hoped. The skill with which it had been composed, and the gesture of fellowship that it made, ensured that the faithful and beleaguered Christians of Germany did not feel excluded from the ecumenical fellowship. That they should still feel themselves part of the *Una Sancta* was to be of incalculable importance in the years ahead.

Bell's hopes for the formation of the World Council of Churches found a genuine measure of fulfilment at Oxford. Life and Work proved ready for the proposed merger with

Faith and Order. The world conference of the latter body meeting a little later at Edinburgh also proved willing, but not without vigorous protest from Headlam, who deeply feared the submerging of the theological side of the ecumennical movement in a council likely to be dominated by what he regarded as the dangerous political concerns of Life and Work. He felt that the latter movement was in grave danger of identifying Christianity with Socialism. He attributed the absence of German delegations from both conferences to the way in which Bell and his colleagues in Life and Work had been interfering in internal affairs in Germany. Of the proposed World Council he wrote: 'If such a Council were to exist and if it passed resolutions on public affairs, it might do a very considerable amount of harm.'[30]

What Headlam did not calculate was what was central in Bell's mind. This was not the potential harm that might be done by interference, but the strong Christian succour which might be given by a world-wide sustaining fellowship of the churches. From 1938 when the 'provisional committee for a World Council of Churches in process of formation' met at Utrecht such a fellowship was in essence in being. Bell was a member of that committee but was absent on that inaugural occasion. The reason was characteristic: he was taking part in Sweden in the consecration to the episcopate of two sons-in-law of his old ecumenical father-in-God, Nathan Söderblom. Such an act was one of deliberate honour to the memory of the man who yearned for such a World Council. From Oxford onwards Bell moved steadily to the heart of the life of that council, and with him took the spiritual power and stature given by his discerning and courageous stand against an idolatry of evil that directly threatened the freedom of Christ's Church.

NOTES

1. See G. K. A. Bell, *The Church and Humanity* (*1939–1946*). Longmans 1946, p. 67.

2. *The Stockholm Conference*, pp. 712–713.

3. Ehrenström, Rouse-Neill, p. 585.

4. *The Kingship of Christ*, p. 30.

5. See Eberhard Bethge, *Dietrich Bonhoeffer*, Collins 1970, pp. 398–400 (later referred to as Bethge).

6. Bethge, p. 206.

7. Mary Bosanquet, *Dietrich Bonhoeffer*, Hodder & Stoughton 1968, pp. 127–128 (later referred to as Bosanquet).

8. Dietrich Bonhoeffer, *No Rusty Swords*, ed. E. H. Robertson, Collins 1965, p. 283.

9. SCM Press. Second, revised edition 1967. An enlarged and definitive edition is to be published in the autumn of 1971.

10. Bethge, p. 49.

11. Bosanquet, p. 135. For the early correspondence between Bell and Bonhoeffer see *No Rusty Swords*, pp. 254–260.

12. Theodore Gill, *Memo for a Movie*, SCM Press 1971, p. 65.

13. Quoted in Bethge, p. 242.

14. Ehrenström, Rouse-Neill, p. 560

15. Quoted in Jasper, p. 105.

16. *No Rusty Swords*, pp. 267–268, gives the whole letter.

17. Quoted in Bosanquet, pp. 140–141.

18. Quoted in Bethge, p. 297.

19. *The Kingship of Christ*, p. 30.

20. Ehrenström, Rouse-Neill, p. 593.

21. Marc Boegner, *The Long Road to Unity*, Collins 1970, p. 78.

22. Minutes of the meeting of the Council, Fanö, pp. 51 f.; quoted in Bethge, p. 307.

23. Quoted in Ehrenström, Rouse-Neill, p. 583.

24. See Bethge, pp. 308–309.

25. Jasper, pp. 118–119.

26. *The Long Road to Unity*, p. 75.

27. Jasper, pp. 207–208.

28. Quoted in Bethge, p. 455.

29. Canon Jasper has given accounts of this conflict in his official biographies of both protagonists. See *Arthur Cayley Headlam*, Faith Press 1960, pp. 290–301, and *Bell*, pp. 218–230.

30. *Headlam*, p. 276.

5   A Lonely Leader in War-time

When war came there were three British Christian leaders who exerted great influence on the European scene. They were William Temple, Archbishop of York, William Paton, leader in the work of the International Missionary Council and a joint general secretary of the World Council of Churches 'in process of formation', and George Bell. Paton seems almost to have become the forgotten man of the ecumenical movement, but Archbishop Garbett wrote of him, 'If he had been an Anglican he would have been one of the Archbishops',[1] and when that Presbyterian missionary statesman died his memorial service was in St Paul's Cathedral with the Archbishop of Canterbury giving the address. He will appear in the story to be told in this chapter, but he was chiefly a 'back-room boy' of the ecumenical movement, and had no office apt to catch the attention of the wider public. His influence in Europe was quietly along the lines of ecumenical communication.

Temple was a towering figure who had shared deeply in virtually all the streams of ecumenical activity. He had a massive and international intellectual reputation. He had remarkable facility of speech, and a power of bringing out material from the abundant stores of his mind immediately on demand. His personality, and a rare gift for eirenical speech without lapsing into superficiality, added to all these other gifts, made him unique in reputation amongst church leaders. No other man could be contemplated as president of the World Council of Churches. (It was a tribute to him that when that Council was fully formed, and he was dead, a presidium of six was set up, rather than the single presidency which he would have filled.)

Bell's influence in Europe was of a different sort from either Paton's or Temple's. He held an ancient and high office, if one with less prestige than Temple's, but the influence was in every sense deeply personal. He had been involved, first as Davidson's 'eyes and ears' and then by his own standing, in all the significant meetings of Life and Work since Oud Wassenaar in 1919. During those twenty years he had emerged to undisputed leadership of that side of the ecumenical movement. It was the leadership of a man most personally and spiritually committed to the work. There was nothing whatever of the highly placed churchman merely fulfilling an office as his share of the work to be done. The whole of his eager, if shy, spirit was engaged in this. He revelled in the opportunities it brought him of widening circles of friendship with those of other nations and of very different Christian traditions. He was not an ecumenist because the twentieth century was an ecumenical century and therefore he played his due part, but because he had been captured by a vision. This was a vision of the *Una Sancta*, the one Christian fellowship which transcends all human divisions. But it was also a vision of a humanity which was called to realize its oneness. Since Bell died much has been heard (especially since the fourth assembly of the World Council of Churches held at Uppsala in 1968) of the need for the ecumenical movement to stress not an ecclesiastical ecumenism but a human ecumenism. Bell would have taken the point, but it is possible to imagine the gently bewildered look that would have crossed his face at the suggestion that this emphasis was some new discovery. What else had inspired Söderblom, the great man of Uppsala? What else had been the driving force of his own life from the Stockholm conference onwards? It was not for nothing that he called the volume of his war-time speeches and articles, *The Church and Humanity*.

It was not a generalized humanity. It was actual individual persons. In this way, too, was his ecumenical leadership deeply personal. Not only did he give the whole of himself, that almost remorseless industry, that steely will, that commitment grounded in profound and regular devotional habit, but he gave it to individuals all the time. If any man could have claimed intolerable burdens of work to excuse him from over-much concern with individuals he could, for the work of his diocese and his involvement in wider Anglican affairs would have over-filled the time of most men. To all that he added the leadership in time of crisis that the last chapter has only sketched in outline. His letters to Bonhoeffer reveal the need to fit in some essential consultation over breakfast at the Athenaeum. His days, and too often too many hours of the night, were mortgaged to meeting the relentless demands of his work and his wider concerns at a level of preparation that satisfied the man who had been the senior chaplain at Lambeth in Davidson's day. (A day, incidentally, when the customary long holidays of such leaders were still uninvaded by weeks of ecumenical meetings.)

It seems never to have occurred to Bell that all this gave any reason for him to be defended from the demands of individuals upon him. Perhaps he remembered what he had recorded in his life of Davidson. Sir Thomas Barlow, Davidson's physician, had read the Archbishop a little homily which ended, 'There are only twenty-four hours in the day. If you are so ready to help Tom, Dick and Harry in their small matters it will be physically impossible for you to attend to the weightier matters of the law.' Davidson's reply was, 'Well, I can only tell you that such help as

I could give to Tom, Dick and Harry, as you call them, has helped me to give counsel in the weightier matters of the law.'[2] Such personal engagement was, in any case, natural to Bell. We have seen how the base of all his deeply informed leadership in the German church struggle was his friendship with the young Bonhoeffer. It was friendship in every way, not a working relationship warmed by a certain regard.

When war came the nature of his leadership was to impart both strength and weakness to his stand. The fact that his convictions were rooted in the heart of his being, and above all in his belief that Jesus of Nazareth was the saviour of all men, meant that unpopularity and national and social pressures counted for little. He was too experienced an ecclesiastic not to know that his stand would almost certainly bar the road to promotion for him, and too 'establishment' in temper of mind to discount that too readily; but at no point at all is there any suggestion of trimming or wavering. He kept his course, and no tempest of patriotic indignation could blow him off it.

There remained some weakness: it was the kind of weakness which is honourable to a Christian man and leader. Because his emotions were so deeply engaged in the fate of his friends it was not always easy for him to recognize the obdurate necessities of war. His own perception of the true nature of National Socialism, and the way in which it had resisted every external influence towards retaining a measure of freedom, or some vestiges of civilized behaviour, revealed the necessity of war; but he was like David in his instructions to his commanders in combatting the rebellion of Absalom, his son. Love warred against resolution. For him Germany was the fetid centre of an evil that threatened the world, but it was also the home of Martin Niemöller (even if the evil had cast him into a concentration camp), of Praeses Koch, who treasured right through the war years Bell's letter to him,[3] and above all of his beloved Dietrich Bonhoeffer. As war became certain Bonhoeffer, who was in New York, became convinced that he must return to Germany. He had written to Reinhold Niebuhr:

> Christians in Germany will face the terrible alternative of either willing the defeat of their nation in order that Christian civilization may survive, or willing the victory of their nation and thereby destroying our civilization. I know which of these alternatives I must choose; but I cannot make that choice in security.[4]

On his way through London he wrote to Bell on 22 July 1939. Even if war miraculously did not come, his passport expired in the following spring and its renewal was most doubtful. So he wrote:

> Let me thank you today for all help and friendship and real understanding in the past and in the future. We shall never forget you during the coming events.[5]

All Bell's German friends received a message saying that nothing that came about could break the unity that they had in Christ. His last letter as war came was to Bonhoeffer.

> My dear Dietrich,
>
> You know how deeply I feel for you and yours in this melancholy time. May God comfort and guide you. I think often of our talk in the summer. May he keep you. Let us pray together by reading the Beatitudes. *Pax Dei superat omnia nos custodiat.*
>
> Yours affectionately,
>
> GEORGE.[6]

We have noted more than once that Bell, in a sense, fulfilled ecclesiastically the role that Churchill fulfilled nationally. Both saw clearly what Nazism was and what Nazism meant. Neither Bell's solid background in the ecclesiastical establishment, nor Churchill's aristocratic and moneyed connections, clouded the penetration of their vision. They were alike in their persistence and in their unpopularity, certainly in Germany, but also in some circles in Britain. There the similarity ends. When war came Churchill had no inhibitions of any kind deriving from love of individual German people. He could and did create an undisturbed stereotype of a nation that must be utterly crushed if civilization were to survive. Being a man of remarkable stature that stereotype did not survive the war in his mind, and he was capable of manifest generosity of spirit after victory. But only after victory. Bell was weakened both by a Chamberlain-like horror of war itself (derived probably, as has been suggested, from the death of so many of his contemporaries, including two of his own brothers, in the first world war), and also by a profound personal affection for many German friends.

But Bell's apparent weakness derived not just from emotion but from knowledge. He *knew*, most intimately but far from exclusively, through his friendship with Bonhoeffer, that there was another Germany. He knew that there were some of the best in the German nation who willed the defeat of their nation in order that civilization might survive. Churchill not only did not possess that knowledge, but would have found it beyond belief if he had. Thus if Churchill stands for realism of one kind, Bell certainly stands for realism of another.

Bell did not in any way dissent from the decision to go to war. In the preface to the book containing the collection of his war-time speeches and articles he wrote:

> I spoke and I wrote as a lover of my country: as a convinced and public opponent of Hitler and the Nazis from the beginning of his dominion as Chancellor of the Reich in 1933; as one who abhors cruelty and barbarism such as Hitler and his followers practised for so long; and as a profound believer in the ideals of liberty and justice in defence of which Great Britain went to war.[7]

But did he see fully the need for that war to go on until Hitler and all he stood for had been dethroned? Some doubt is cast on this, for example, by the account recently published by Marc Boegner of the war-time meeting in January 1940 of the administrative committee of the embryonic World Council of Churches. Even before that Boegner had received a letter from Bell which had disturbed him. His note made at the time reads:

> Letter from my dear friend the Bishop of Chichester. His attitude in favour of negotiations as early as possible seems to me most dangerous. He sends me the report of a disconcerting meeting in the House of Lords during which he spoke in support, on the whole, of accepting the offer of the good offices of the King of the Belgians and the Queen of Holland. . . . Chichester says that he has a sense of reality, but I fear that he may be allowing himself to be over-influenced by German refugees.[8]

The administrative committee met under icy and isolated conditions at Apeldoorn, as guests of some wealthy people who were members of what was then known as the Oxford Group movement. Had this fact been known, bearing in mind the notorious panegyric in praise of Hitler uttered by Frank Buchman, the founder of the movement, much more sinister influences might have been seen at work in the tendency of some in the group to take the line that Bell had done in the Lords. The group included among others Temple, Archbishop Eidem of Uppsala, Bishop Berggrav of Oslo, Visser 't Hooft and Paton. In the complex discussions Bell found full support for his position, according to Boegner, only from Eidem and the British Methodist, Henry Carter, who was a pacifist.

The discussions on a plea for a negotiated peace took place at a preliminary gathering before the administrative committee proper met. Berggrav was their instigator, and the Scandinavian churches as a whole felt their responsibility to fulfil the role of reconcilers. The four British

81

participants signed a statement drawn up by Temple, and this was later published in the British press,[9] but the administrative committee as a whole was unable to agree.

This was, of course, the period of the 'phoney' war, and Christian men might well feel in such a period a particular obligation to redeem the time by efforts at reconciliation. Moreover, Bell was in so many things, as has been emphasized, Söderblom's heir, that he was virtually bound to follow him in tireless efforts towards bringing war to an end. The tragedy of the first world war breaking out amongst supposedly Christian nations had been one of the chief, if not the chief, spring that motivated Söderblom in bringing the Life and Work movement into being. The question must still remain whether Bell, who had had almost unique opportunity amongst non-German churchmen to assess the worth of any promise emerging from Hitler and his gang, was wise to give his support to pleas for a negotiated peace before Hitler had been overthrown. This is a wholly different issue from that which was more seriously to arise later – whether terms other than unconditional surrender should be given to a Germany which had removed Hitler and the Nazis from power. He could rightly claim, 'If long-sustained and public opposition to Hitler and the Nazis is any credential, I would humbly claim to be one of the most convinced and consistent anti-Nazis in Great Britain;'[10] but how did he reconcile this with a plea for a negotiated peace which would leave the Nazis in control? There was a contradiction here, and it was one which was bound to weaken the far more realistic pleas that Bell was to make in the years that followed the outbreak of the 'real' war in May 1940.

Just a few weeks after war broke out Bell stated the creed which was to inspire him throughout the war in an article in the *Fortnightly Review*.[11] Some articles that were written, as this must have been, at the very moment that war broke out would scarcely stand being reprinted when the grim years were over. It is the measure of Bell's solidity of conviction that he could reprint it in 1946, and it can be read as setting out the principles which underlay the whole of his war-time activity. It was on 'The Church's Function in War-time'. He asked what it was and gave a simple but comprehensive answer: 'I am going to urge in this article that it is the function of the Church at all costs to remain the Church.' There was an echo here of the rallying-cry that emerged from the Oxford conference, 'Let the Church be the Church.'

He saw clearly that there was grave danger that the exigencies of war would exact from the church the very sacrifice which must not be made, for it would be of the principle for which the war was being fought. He knew that all the resources of the state would be bound to be concentrated on winning the war, but boldly asserted that the church was not part of those resources. 'It possesses an authority independent of the State.' (What else had been fundamentally at issue in the German church struggle?)

As important was the right and duty of the church to continue to recognize its nature as a fellowship to transcend national divisions. War did not declare a moratorium upon ecumenism. 'The Church in any country fails to be the Church if it forgets that its members in one nation have a fellowship with its members in every nation.'

Finally he declared that right to prophesy which must be claimed by the Christian leader and the Christian community no less in war than in peace.

The Church must guard and maintain . . . moral principles in the war itself. It must not hesitate, if occasion arises, to condemn the infliction of reprisals, or the bombing of civilian populations, by the military forces of its own nation. It should set itself against the propaganda of lies and hatred. It should be ready to encourage a resumption of friendly relations with the enemy nation. It should set its face against any war of extermination or enslavement, and any measures directly aimed at destroying the morale of a population.

Here, in a sense, was his programme. He fulfilled every part of it. He did not see it as a programme, but as a commission. The statesmen who would mistake him for a meddling ecclesiastic, dabbling in politics at a peculiarly dangerous time, totally mistook the man. He was no amateur meddling in politics; he was a man of God determined to see how the gospel might be applied amidst the moral ambiguities of war, and above all how the church, the one divine community, might be the church. It was a position always open to easy demolition by the logician. In willing the destruction of the evil that Nazism represented, why did he shrink from willing the means by which it might be destroyed? Did he not recognize the consequences of the prophetic stance that he himself had taken up? His kind of witness had none of the logical strength of the pacifist; but he would have claimed that his was in the end a truer realism than that of his critics during the war.

Always Bell's concern was a concern for persons. Long before the care of refugees came to have an acknowledged claim upon the concern and action of Christians he was busy trying to stir his own church and others into responding to the needs of those who fled from Nazi Germany. The slowness of the churches to be so stirred is one of the less happy aspects of the story of British Christianity in the pre-war years. When the *blitzkreig* across the Low Countries and France, and the withdrawal of the British armies from the continent, led to a desperate fear that a Fifth Column might exist in Britain – a Britain virtually certain to be invaded – almost panic-stricken measures were taken to intern those of German nationality. Amongst those whisked off in a moment to conditions that were primitive and worse at Huyton in Lancashire, and to the Isle of Man, were many who had already suffered at the hands of Hitler. They now found that they had come to a precarious place of refuge. Bell was valiant in making their plight known, at a time when perhaps this country came nearest to something of that anti-German hysteria which informed sections of the population in the first world war.

On 6 August 1940 he spoke in the Lords on the internment of aliens. It was a speech which rested upon the sure ground of having himself visited the men who were suffering. In Canon Jasper's long biography three of the most moving pages are formed by the descriptions of what his visit meant. One is written by Franz Hildebrandt, Niemöller's colleague and Bonhoeffer's friend, himself a victim of the Aryan Clause.

> He (Bell) could only stammer and stutter. It was an unforgettable moment. The sight of the refugees in their new captivity was just too much for him – it was not only just the question of a wrong to so many of his personal friends, it was a moral burden on the English people. . . . On returning from the Isle of Man he called on the central postal censorship office in Liverpool, inspected the stacked post bags of the past six or eight weeks for which the internees had waited in vain, and suggested quietly but firmly that the letters might be delivered to the people to whom they were addressed. Three days later the camp post office was inundated, and we knew whom we had to thank. Now the writing began from our side: my wife is ill, please tell the Bishop of Chichester; I need a new pair of shoes, please tell the Bishop of Chichester.[12]

The remarkable record is that Bell in the middle of his fantastically busy life, with nothing ever scamped, found time to see to all the practical needs to which his attention was brought, and imagination to foresee many so that they were attended to even before word came to him. Always his concern was not for the refugee problem, but for refugees – men and women who became known to him, and for whom he would go to infinite trouble to establish them in a worthwhile life and a restored happiness.

His stand on behalf of the refugees and his firm assertion of the supra-national character of Christ's church had not in the early years of war brought him into that conflict with the authorities which marked the later years. In early 1942 when the government was trying to maintain contact and influence with Sweden, the one Scandinavian country not overrun by Hitler, by sending leading figures in the cultural life of Britain on official visits there, Bell was the natural choice among church leaders. (Sir Kenneth Clark and T. S. Eliot were sent as representing other aspects of British life.) Bell was, of course, the natural choice. Only Headlam had similar contacts with European churchmen, and he was now eighty, deaf, and (we may suppose) somewhat discredited as an apologist for Hitler. Bell was a personal friend of Archbishop Eidem of Uppsala, and well known at many points of Swedish church life.

On 13 May he made the somewhat hazardous flight to Stockholm, the city where his ecumenical leadership had begun over quarter of a century before. For almost three weeks he discharged his appointed duties, making contacts with many old friends and radiating his own special brand of confidence that the future was safe in the hands of God. It was not a confidence based on some eupeptic and superficial view of events, but on his faith. He had expressed it some months before war broke out, when he was honoured by an invitation from the Jewish Historical Society of England to give the Lucien Wolf Memorial Lecture[13] to the society:

> . . . justice, mercy, liberty will re-assert their sway. The oppression will cease, as it has ceased before. Belief in God, and the lessons of history, forbid us to despair.

There may have been something of the old-fashioned

Victorian liberal in that reference to the lessons of history, but that was the lesser, far the lesser, ground of his confidence. To read his war-time speeches is to appreciate the degree to which he felt secure in his position because of the rock on which he had built his convictions. That rock was Christ, and the revelation of the nature of God and his purpose that Christ had made. Nothing could be more misleading than any suggestion that politics and international issues were the heart of Bell's life. They were areas where obedience had to be offered to that Lord who was the centre of his being. It was for this reason that his sanctity had that trying obstinacy which always irritates worldly men.

His dutiful discharge of his task must have brought him joy in the renewal of friendships. Certainly it gave him an exhilarating opportunity to breathe again the larger air of international ecumenical relationships, and the chance to assess the role of the church in the post-war situation from a vantage point less immured than beleaguered Britain. He gave Christians the benefit of his reflections through the medium of Dr J. H. Oldham's *Christian News-Letter*[14] during the following month.

That account, however, of necessity omitted the most dramatic and unexpected side of his experience. It was on that officially-sponsored visit to Sweden that Bell touched the fringes of history, and provided one of the most fascinating 'might have beens' of our era. On 26 May Bell was taken to the Student Movement House in Stockholm by Nils Ehrenström (from whose account of the history of the Life and Work movement many quotations have already been made in this book). There he was startled to find Dr Hans Schönfeld, who was director of the research department at Geneva which was Life and Work's most significant day-to-day work. Schönfeld had come deliberately to Sweden from Geneva, via Germany, because Bell was there. He revealed that he had come to make contact on behalf of elements in Germany which were seeking the overthrow of Hitler. Five days later when Bell was at the famous ecumenical centre, Sigtuna, an even more startling, and very joyous, encounter ensued. Dietrich Bonhoeffer arrived unannounced, having learned from Visser 't Hooft during a visit to Geneva that his English father-in-God was in Sweden, and therefore their deep friendship could be renewed. But renewal of friendship was not the sole or chief purpose of Bonhoeffer's swift journey to Sweden. He, too, came as an emissary of elements in the German resistance, wholly independent of Schönfeld, who did not in general command Bonhoeffer's confidence. He was considered to be somewhat ambivalent in his ecclesiastical loyalties, since he both loyally served Life and Work as a staff member and maintained contact with Bishop Heckel and the official side of the German Evangelical Church.

In his biography of Bonhoeffer, Eberhard Bethge has carefully listed the sources in Bell's own writing which may be drawn upon for any reconstruction of those remarkable days in Sweden in May and June 1942.[15] The list of them indicates not only the measure of importance that Bonhoeffer has come to have in the Christian history of our time, but the significance that Bell attached to the initiative taken so perilously, and in the end so fruitlessly, by those two German pastors.

At the first meeting Schönfeld, revealing the deep sense of strain that he was experiencing, told Bell of the plans being made by a strong and organized resistance movement within Germany for the destruction of the Nazi regime. The purpose of his contact with the English bishop was to find out through him whether success on the part of that resistance might lead to the possibility of a negotiated peace.

It is important to stress that Bell, for all the enthusiasm which he had shown during the 'phoney' war period at the Apeldoorn meeting for a negotiated peace, did not show the faintest naïvete in responding to this overture. Schönfeld had given an impressive account of a resistance made up of three main elements, members or former members of the state administration, large numbers of key trade unionists in the main industrial centres like Berlin, Hamburg and Cologne, and highly placed officers both in the army and the police. Schönfeld also set out in detail the principles upon which a reordered Germany would be based, if this resistance were able to effect what was seen to be the essential first step, the elimination of Hitler.[16] But Schönfeld was not a figure who inspired full confidence. His links with Heckel had been rather close. Bell acquainted his host, the British Minister in Stockholm, Mr Victor Mallet (as he then was), with the approach. The Minister was very cautious, suspecting that this was a disguised peace feeler.

At the second meeting with Schönfeld, on 29 May, the German pastor stressed more fully even than at the meeting three days earlier the basically Christian character of the resistance movement that he represented.

Indeed, most of Dr Schönfeld's conversation on this occasion was devoted to stating what the Churches had done, advocating the necessity of a Christian basis of government, and pointing out the significance in relation to Germany of the Church opposition in Holland and Norway.[17]

This was the best of all grounds for an appeal to Bell, but far more compelling was an appeal from a man whom he could totally trust. This came, as it must have appeared quite incredibly, when two days later Bonhoeffer arrived at Sigtuna. Bell had yearned that his visit to neutral territory might afford the opportunity to renew his friendship with the young German. 'I wish I could see Dietrich there', he had written, just before leaving, to Bonhoeffer's refugee brother-in-law. Through Archbishop Eidem he had tried to find out Bonhoeffer's movements, but failed.[18] It seemed unlikely that one so marked as Bonhoeffer could be expected to arrive in a neutral country, but he was in fact already playing that dangerous game as a 'double agent of the *Abwehr*' which in its complexity would require a John le Carré to have justice done to it.

Bonhoeffer was able to confirm all that Schönfeld had said. The independence of his own approach, and the degree to which he had parted company with Schönfeld in the past reinforced the confirmation that he gave. Here, above all, in Bonhoeffer was a man whom Bell knew could be trusted through and through. In the brief interval between the second talk with Schönfeld and the visit to Sigtuna, Bell had been to Uppsala and talked about Schönfeld's approach to his old friend Archbishop Eidem. Eidem fully believed in Schönfeld's sincerity, but gave less credence to his facts. He thought that there was some indulgence in wishful thinking, and that Schönfeld had relieved his feelings about the tragedy in his own land by pouring out all his hopes to one whom he knew would sympathize.

Bonhoeffer countered this by being willing to reveal the names of the leaders in the German resistance. Here were no vague groups, no matter how grandly described, but actual people whom a wholly trustworthy man, of proved sound judgment, could firmly state to adhere to the cause of the overthrow of Hitler. In a later account of the whole incident, which Bell gave in a lecture in Gottingen in 1957,[19] he recorded how he had warned his friend of the suspicion with which the British government was bound to treat the whole approach, and how greatly it would help if names could be given.

He agreed readily – although I could see that there was a heavy load on his mind about the whole affair. He named Col.-General Beck, Col.-General von Hammerstein, former chiefs of the General Staff, Herr Goedeler, former Lord Mayor of Leipzig, Wilhelm Leuscher, former President of the United Trade Unions, Jacob Kaiser, Catholic Trade Union leader. He also mentioned Schacht, as an ambiguous supporter, a 'seismograph of contemporary events'.

This was an impressive list. It was accompanied by the assurance that most of the field marshals and generals were reliable from the point of view of the conspirators.

There was another way in which Bonhoeffer's approach was more compelling than that of his fellow pastor. When Bell and Bonhoeffer stopped their private talk and were joined by others, including Schönfeld, the latter expounded his ideas, notably in regard to Russia.

Here Bonhoeffer broke in (said Bell at Göttingen). His Christian conscience, he said, was not quite at ease with Schönfeld's ideas. There must be punishment by God. We should not be worthy of such a solution. Our action must be such as the world will understand as an act of repentance. 'Christians do not wish to escape repentance, or chaos, if it is God's will to bring it upon us. We must take this judgment as Christians.' When Bonhoeffer spoke of the importance of the Germans declaring their repentance, I expressed very strong agreement with him. I also spoke of the importance of the Allied armies occupying Berlin. Schönfeld agreed to this, but with the proviso that they occupied Berlin not as conquerors but to assist the German Army against reactionary or hostile forces.

The distance that Bell had moved since 1940 can be seen in his insistence that the Allied armies must occupy Berlin. Now that the war had run more than two and a half years of its course he was clear that such occupation was necessary. This conviction is to be borne in mind when we turn to the speeches that he made in criticism of the bombing policy of the Allies, and his struggle to move the government away from a sterile policy of demanding unconditional surrender. He had now every reason to believe in the existence of a determined and influential German resistance.

Nothing would have put more heart into such men, living and plotting in daily danger of their lives, than the assurance that a Germany which had overthrown Hitler and his crew would be differently treated from a Nazi Germany driven to total defeat.

The question was: could Bell secure such assurance? Code messages were agreed before they parted in which Bell could give news of the response of the British government. A letter from Bonhoeffer came to Bell before he left Stockholm.

> It still seems to me like a dream to have seen you, to have spoken to you, to have heard your voice. I think these days will remain in my memory as some of the greatest of my life. The spirit of fellowship and of Christian brotherliness will carry me through the darkest hours, and even if things go worse than we hope and expect, the light of these few days will never extinguish in my heart. The impressions of these days were so overwhelming that I cannot express them in words.[20]

Bell, on his return, saw Anthony Eden, the Foreign Secretary. Eden was deeply interested, not least in the list of names with which Bell had been supplied by Bonhoeffer. He did not doubt the sincerity of the pastors, but was inclined to think that they were unconsciously being used to put out peace feelers. Such feelers had been out in Turkey and Madrid (a surprising circumstance when the military dominance of Germany at the time is considered). 'He (Eden) must be scrupulously careful not to enter even into the appearance of negotiations with the enemy, and be able to say truthfully that this was so, both to Russia and to America.'[21]

Bell also went to see Sir Stafford Cripps, a devout Christian who had been a leading figure in the World Alliance for the Promotion of International Friendship through the Churches. Cripps had talked with Visser 't Hooft during the previous month, who had shown him and left with him a memorandum by Adam von Trott, who had been suggested as a possible intermediary by the two German pastors. Cripps was impressed by this and showed it to Churchill. He was also impressed with Schönfeld's statement and promised to talk it over with Eden. Eden caused the Foreign Office to examine all parallel information, but gave his firm answer in a letter written on 4 August:

I am very conscious of the importance of what you say about not discouraging any elements of opposition in Germany to the Nazi regime. You will remember that in my speech at Edinburgh on May 8th I devoted quite a long passage to Germany and concluded by saying that, if any section of the German people really wished to see a return to a German state based on respect for law and the rights of the individual, they must understand that no one would believe them until they had taken active steps to rid themselves of their present regime.

For the present I do not think that it would be advisable to go any further in a public statement. I realize the dangers and difficulties to which the opposition in Germany is exposed, but they have so far given little evidence of their existence and until they show that they are willing to follow the example of the oppressed peoples of Europe in running risks and taking active steps to oppose and overthrow the Nazi rule of terror, I do not see how we can usefully expand the statements which have already been made by members of the Government about Germany. I think those statements have made it quite clear that we do not intend to deny Germany a place in the future Europe, but that the longer the German people tolerate the Nazi regime, the greater becomes their responsibility for the crimes which that regime is committing in their name.[22]

While naturally revealing nothing of the conversations that had taken place in Sweden, Bell raised the whole question of encouragement to those Germans who desired the overthrow of Hitler in an important speech in the Lords on 10 March 1943. His intimate knowledge of the German church struggle had taught him with what peril any man or any body sought to oppose the Hitlerite state.

But in spite of the cruelty and murder and of the paralysing effect – paralysing physically, psychologically, morally – of the ruthless strategy of the Nazis' oppression, vast numbers of the German people refused to bow the kneee to Baal. . . . When we are tempted to blame the German people for their docility, we must remember the multitude of assassins and spies.[23]

While Lord Simon, replying to the debate, gave assurance that the destruction of the Hitlerite state did not imply that the whole German people was doomed to destruction, the word of encouragement to the German resistance was never spoken, and certainly no aid was given to it such as buttressed and equipped the resistance in occupied territories.

The truth behind the approach of the two German pastors was proved tragically. On 20 July 1944 the plot to assassinate Hitler failed. The conspirators were ruthlessly exterminated. Churchill could scornfully dismiss the whole affair as 'the highest personalities in the German Reich murdering one another', but the list of those who died at Hitler's enraged orders corresponded with the list that Bonhoeffer had given to Bell at Sigtuna. The resistance was a reality. It had pursued its purpose without any encouragement, and thus proved its integrity. There was doubtless a mixture of motives, but the calibre of many who had joined in the desperate plot showed that it was Christian faith and human idealism that provided the mainspring of the abortive attempt to rid Germany and the world of the evil Führer.

By now Bell had become engaged on another front of conflict with the British government. Here he was judged to be not misguided and deceived (as many must have thought him to be in his pleas for 'the other Germany'), but positively dangerous and weakening to the war effort. This new front was the bombing policy being pursued against German cities.

On 9 February 1944 he spoke in the Lords on the issue of obliteration bombing. The heart of his well-informed and cogently argued speech lay in these words:

It is no longer definite military and industrial objectives which are the aim of the bombers, but the whole town, area by area, is plotted carefully out. This area is singled out and plastered on one night; that area is singled out and plastered on another night; a third, a fourth, a fifth area is similarly singled out and plastered night after night, till, to use the language of the Chief of Bomber Command with regard to Berlin, the heart of Nazi Germany ceases to beat. How can there be discrimination in such matters when civilians, monuments, military objectives and industrial objectives all together form the target? How can the bombers aim at anything more than a great space when they see nothing and the bombing is blind?[24]

This was not the first time he had raised this issue, although it was by far the most public occasion. In the previous September he had written about it in such terms in his own *Diocesan Gazette* as to arouse bitter protests throughout his diocese. The protests led his friend the Dean, A. S. Duncan-Jones, to ask him to withdraw from preaching in his own cathedral at a service to commemorate the third anniversary of the Battle of Britain. His Lords speech, however, was intended as a challenge to the nation. It had been vetted by the outstanding military strategist of the day, Captain Liddell Hart, and therefore was unchallengeable on its facts. Interestingly, Canon Jasper reveals that Bell had the support of his old opponent Headlam of Gloucester in making it.

It created a remarkable furore, with the expected apoplectic explosions from papers such as *The Daily Telegraph* and the *Daily Mail*, but moderate assessments in more thoughtful quarters in the secular press, and some relief expressed in the religious press that a Christian leader had spoken about an issue that was nagging the conscience of thoughtful Christians. Although his war-time speeches were concerned with many aspects of the struggle, and perhaps most notably with the absence of any 'weapon of the idea' (to use his own phrase) in the British offensive, it was that speech on obliteration bombing which was most identified with him.

His own official biographer is critical of his stance at this point, while seeing his stand as noble and far from useless. He makes the comment on Bell's later condemnation of the use of the atomic bomb against Japan:

This final protest revealed as clearly as any the intellectual weakness of Bell's position. Fundamentally he believed that war was wrong – 'War is destructive, and war not only wastes life and wastes material resources, but poisons human relationships.' Yet he refused to become a pacifist. . . . As the struggle dragged on, he deplored the retreat from the original high ideals; yet the war itself made such a retreat inevitable. His sensitive conscience therefore made him a constant critic of government policy, but it also forced him into a dilemma which did not make for logic and consistency.[25]

Against this comment may be put the firm defence of Bell by his friend and former chaplain, the present Archdeacon of Chichester, Lancelot Mason.

The one over-riding principle in the conduct of the war must be the defeat of the enemy. But does that mean that in time of war the Church must be silent about Christian principles? That its only function in wartime is to bless the nation's weapons of war and pray for the annihilation of the enemy? It was one of Bishop Bell's main arguments that the Church must at all times, in war as in peace be the Church. . . . It must speak to men of love, even of the love of one's enemy. Is a war worth fighting, is it worth winning, if at the end of it you have reduced your own people to the same level of evil against which they took up arms?[26]

In strict logic no Christian stance in time of war is defensible. The pacifist even in eating benefits from the armed forces that have guarded the convoys which brought him his food. He finds himself protesting against vile evil, such as Nazism, yet refusing to will any clear means for its defeat. The man who like Bell refuses the pacifist position can always be accused of wanting to fight war with gentility. But it is perhaps far more perceptive to read his position as Professor Donald Mackinnon reads it: 'Bell's greatness in a measure corresponded to Bonhoeffer's: the master lived out in his own very different situation the moral and spiritual tensions articulated by the theologian, prophet, and martyr whose mentor he was.'[27]

When the July plot failed Bonhoeffer was already in prison. He was hanged on the express orders of Hitler at Flossenbürg just before the war ended. The meeting in Sweden was to be the last between the two friends. Bonhoeffer's last message as he was taken out to execution, sent through a British prisoner, was to the English bishop who had been his friend from the first months that he engaged in the Christian struggle against the monstrous evil of Nazism.

> Tell him (he said) that for me this is the end but also the beginning –
> with him I believe in the principle of our Universal Christian brother-
> hood which rises above all national interests, and that our victory
> is certain – tell him too that I have never forgotten his words at our
> last meeting.[28]

Strangely, it was through the broadcast of a memorial service that the Bishop conducted in London for his friend that the Bonhoeffer family learned that Dietrich was dead. Bell had learned through Geneva, but the disorder and confusion in Berlin was still too great for the news to have come through. At the service he spoke of the possibility of resurrection for the church through the leadership of men like Bonhoeffer. There was 'for the Church, not only in that Germany which he loved, but the Church Universal which was greater to him than nations, the hope of a new life'.[29] It was a strange echo of the last words of his younger friend, which had not yet reached him.

Three months later Bell led the first post-war deputation of English churchmen to Berlin. He visited the Bonhoeffer family. Professor Gordon Rupp has described the scene.

> And now his mother went to a drawer and took from it a little book
> from which her son had made his devotions in his last imprisonment.
> And as the bishop took it from her and kissed the old lady on her

forehead, he held up the volume so that the afternoon light fell on its title, *The Imitation of Christ*.[30]

Whatever inconsistencies and illogicalities his stand during the war had revealed, it had had one underlying compulsion, to see how Christ could be imitated amidst the moral ambiguities and hideous complexities of modern war. 'In one dark land at least', reflected Professor Rupp as he saw the precious gift made, 'this Englishman, with his clear blue eyes, has been in our time an emblem of Christian truth, justice and divine compassion in shining armour, a very gentle knight.'[30]

NOTES

1. Charles Smyth, *Cyril Forster Garbett*, Hodder & Stoughton 1959, p. 460

2. *Davidson*, Vol. i, p. 581.

3. See Jasper, p. 242, fn. 23.

4. Dietrich Bonhoeffer, *The Way to Freedom*, ed. E. H. Robertson, Collins 1966, p. 246.

5. *The Way to Freedom*, p. 249.

6. Jasper, p. 243.

7. *The Church and Humanity*, p. v.

8. *The Long Road to Unity*, p. 139. (See subsequent pages for an account of the administrative committee meeting and the consultation on pleas for a negotiated peace which preceded it. A further account can be found in Margaret Sinclair, *William Paton*, SCM Press 1949, pp. 243–239.)

9. See W. A. Visser 't Hooft, 'The Genesis of the World Council of Churches', Rouse-Neill, pp. 708–709.

10. *The Church and Humanity*, p. 129.

11. Reprinted in *The Church and Humanity*, pp. 22–31.

12. Jasper, p. 149.

13. Reprinted in *The Church and Humanity*, pp. 1–21.

14. 24 June 1942, reprinted in *The Church and Humanity*, pp. 70–78.

15. Bethge, p. 664.

16. See Bell's first published account of the encounters in Sweden in an article published in the *Contemporary Review*, October 1945, reprinted in *The Church and Humanity*, pp. 165–176.

17. *The Church and Humanity*, p. 169.

18. Bethge, p. 666.

19. Printed in *I Knew Dietrich Bonhoeffer*, ed. Wolf-Dieter Zimmermann and Ronald Gregor Smith, Collins 1966, pp. 196–211.

20 and 21. *I Knew Dietrich Bonhoeffer*, p. 206 and p. 207.

22. The Earl of Avon, *The Reckoning: The Eden Memoirs*, Cassell 1965, pp, 334–335.

23. *The Church and Humanity*, pp. 98–99.

24. *The Church and Humanity*. pp. 134–135.

25. Jasper, p. 283.

26. Lancelot Mason, ' "Soldiers" and Bishop Bell', *Crucible* (The Journal of the Church Assembly Board of Social Responsibility), March 1969, pp. 35–36.

27. Donald Mackinnon, Letter in *Crucible*, July 1969, p. 123.

28. *I Knew Dietrich Bonhoeffer*, pp. 209–210.

29. Bethge, p. 834.

30 and 31. E. G. Rupp, 'A Great Bishop of Our Time', *The Manchester Guardian*, 12 October 1958.

6 ' . . . Which Was Our Duty to Do'

When the Concertgebouw at Amsterdam filled on 22 August 1948 with the delegates and other representatives of 147 churches come together to inaugurate the World Council of Churches in its fully-organized form, Bell must have reflected with thanksgiving on the degree to which the church had 'been the church' across the war years. Only three years after the end of the most sundering and destructive conflict the nations had known the churches of the world had resolved to enter into this wholly new commitment to one another. The churches from the nations so recently at war were there. His mind went back, as his speech to the opening session revealed, to his first ecumenical gathering, also on Dutch soil, at Oud Wassenaar almost thirty years before. There Söderblom 'had made his momentous proposal for "an Ecumenical Council representing Christendom in a spiritual way" '.[1] It also went back to the Fanö meeting in 1934, that ecumenical gathering which had faced the essence of the challenge that Hitler represented, and what it must mean for the church to be the church.

In the work of the assembly Bell was naturally assigned to Section IV which was appointed to deal with 'The Church and International Disorder'. There was a sharp clash between Bell and John Foster Dulles on the possibility of a 'just' war under modern conditions. Bell wanted the idea rejected, but was also opposed by a young Anglican lay delegate, Quintin Hogg, who now, as Lord Chancellor, presides over the Lords where Bell made his controversial war-time speeches. Bell had the satisfaction of finding his comment on the section's work during the Assembly's debate upon it included in the official report.

A just war was fought for just causes with just means and terminated with a just peace. But a great change occurred in the twentieth century. . . . In the second world war total war became unrestricted war and means were employed that no one could call human – obliteration bombing and the indiscrimate use of atomic force. The distinction between just and unjust war had disappeared. . . . It was time for the Christian Church to urge the world to recognize that harsh fact: that modern war brings barbarism and cannot be an act of justice.[2]

Bell's major task at the assembly, itself a recognition of the great seniority he had come to have, was to chair the policy committee charged with the necessarily delicate arrangements regarding the membership and functions of the newly formed body and many related questions. This recognition made it virtually inevitable that he should be elected chairman of the powerful central committee, consisting of the presidents and ninety other members, which would supervise and direct the work of the council between assemblies. The first meeting of the newly appointed committee took place at Woudschoeten, in Holland, immediately after the assembly, and Bell was duly elected, with Dr Franklin Clark Fry, President of the United Lutheran Church in America, as his vice-chairman.

Fry was a representative figure of the new ecumenical era which had now opened. Two-thirds of the members of the all-important central committee were new to ecumenical experience in any deep sense. Men like Fry, immensely influential leaders of large churches, were essential if the council were truly to be a council of churches and not just a gathering of ecumenical enthusiasts.

It was equally essential that the central committee should itself become a fellowship in which its members gained

101

ecumenical experience and were enlarged by ecumenical vision. This was Bell's supreme contribution in the years of his chairmanship from 1948–1954. I was present at the central committee meeting in Chicago which prefaced the second assembly at Evanston in the latter year. It was clear that in the intervening years this disparate group had been welded into so close a company of friends that some were finding it almost unbearable that they would not meet in that way again (since the forthcoming assembly was rightly bound to make large changes in membership). The company centred on the shy Anglican bishop who was its chairman. This concentration on him was not because he had the obvious gifts to dominate a large group of men and women, themselves almost all accustomed to central places of leadership, but because of the unique spiritual authority that he brought to the work, and his determination that it should be done in a thoroughly Christian manner.

Bell was in fact, by ordinary standards, not a very good chairman. By contrast his vice-chairman, Fry, was superbly gifted in this regard, and at his death had earned the description in a *Times* obituary notice as 'the greatest ecclesiastical parliamentarian of his generation'. Bell relied a great deal upon him, and Fry's self-effacement deserved all praise. Bell's mind was not incisive, and he had more the habit of a bishop presiding over his diocesan conference than of a moderator merely holding the ring. This called for some adjustment on the part of many members of the committee. Dr Robert Mackie comments on the first full meeting of the committee which was held at Chichester itself in the summer of 1949:

Bell's genius for welding a group together had begun, and thereafter the members were gently but firmly directed in the way they should go. At times there were looks of astonishment, even of irritation, in the faces of those who had not met this type of chairmanship before, but for a world body beginning its work it could not have been bettered.[3]

There was something strange, as Robert Mackie also remarks, in the contrast between Bell's humility and informality on the one hand and his pertinacity and courage on the other. Possibly it was only the humility and the hesitant manner which enabled him to get away with the firm leadership which he was in fact exercising. A more obviously masterful man, and one whose manner was confident rather than hesitant, would have aroused strong opposition.

Bell's position was also strengthened enormously by his ecumenical stature. It was not just that he had thirty years of intimate experience of the movement behind him; it was that an Anglo-Saxon, most unusually, commanded the total confidence and indeed the glowing affection of continental Europeans.

It was some of his fellow-Englishmen who were more apt to be critical of his type of ecumenical leadership. Dr Leslie Hunter, then Bishop of Sheffield, who accompanied Bell on a visit by eight churchmen to the British zone of Germany in October 1946, comments that in one sense he was not a leader 'because he was very markedly a man who liked going his own way, and indeed rather enjoyed being in a minority'. On that visit he never discussed with any other members of the team what he was going to say at the big service in Berlin, and since he used the occasion to attack the policy of the British Control Commission before they had their interview with the deputy military governor, this had its embarrassing side. Dr Hunter adds: 'On the other hand, one would balance what I have said with the fact which is quite amazing that as we went round West Germany in 1946 the German churchmen, lay and clerical, regarded him with veneration. It was most remarkable.'[4]

Again, in the organization of that visit he calmly bypassed the British Council of Churches, and when challenged about it said that since it was essential to have Roman Catholic co-operation, and that might not have been easy on a BCC platform, it was essential to do it that way. Dr Oliver Tomkins, now Bishop of Bristol, a member of that team, comments, 'It illustrates his essential pragmatism in reaching goals.'

His dogged purposefulness for good had its undoubted dangers. All men of deep prayer and commitment will have to face the temptation towards a devout and consecrated egotism. Sir Kenneth Grubb, perhaps enjoying a little iconoclasm, in his recent autobiography writes of Bell:

> He was by no means easy to work with. He was a vigorous man of peace, and such men like to have their own way. If he did not secure it, he would go off on his own, ignore his colleagues, and navigate his own canoe, sometimes landing on the rocks.

But even this critic adds that 'His human sympathy was not vague, collective and general, but painstaking and individual . . . His devotion, integrity, capacity for work and taste in the arts and culture generally were beyond criticism.'[5]

It is nevertheless clear that Bell brought to his chairmanship of the central committee during the first six formative years the absolutely essential contribution. He had been indefatigable in the three years between the end of the war and the Amsterdam assembly in knitting together the ecumenical fellowship across the world, and in the six years that followed he made of the new instrument a caring and committed Christian fellowship that was concerned about the central issues.

They were not easy years. On the ecclesiastical front there was the sharp question, not least in Eastern Orthodox minds, of the character of the council itself. Did belonging to it commit the member churches to acknowledgment of all other member bodies as fully churches? It was at the

Toronto meeting in 1950 that the statement 'The Church, the Churches and the World Council of Churches' was hammered out in a committee under the chairmanship of Dr R. D. Whitehorn and warmly welcomed by Bell. It did much to ease the way for that full participation by Orthodoxy that has been so strong a feature of the council's life in recent years.

Far sharper was the question raised by the Korean war, which also fell to be considered at that Toronto meeting. The committee took the bold step of declaring by resolution that an act of aggression had been committed.

> The United Nations Commission in Korea, the most objective witness available, asserts that 'all evidence points to a calculated, co-ordinated attack prepared and launched with secrecy' by the North Korean troops.
>
> Armed attack as an instrument of national policy is wrong. We therefore commend the United Nations, an instrument of world order, for its prompt decision to meet this aggression and for authorizing a police measure which every member nation should support.

This declaration led to the resignation before the committee met in the following year of Dr T. C. Chao, the distinguished Chinese scholar who was the Asian member of the presidium.[6]

They were certainly not easy years, but Bell had the satisfaction of bringing to the second assembly at Evanston, Illinois, in 1954 a united and harmonious central committee that had discharged its tasks with a commendable degree of courage. The World Council was now fully established, and much was owed to Bell for this achievement.

The achievement was recognized by his election at that assembly to the high honour of being Honorary President of the Council. It was intended to mark not only what he had done since Amsterdam, but what he had done since the Stockholm conference almost thirty years before. His participation in the life of the Council, both at the executive and central committees, continued with unabated enthusiasm. At the smaller executive committee Dr Kathleen Bliss remembers this phase:

> He used always to be occupied with his little notebook and with preparing a resolution. He would start on the latter quite early in the proceedings and work on it for a long time, almost always on some international theme. This was usually a good and useful thing, but sometimes his efforts were a bit misplaced and he could be very obstinate about pressing them.[7]

At the last meeting of his life, a central committee at Nyborg, Denmark, it was a mark of his very failing health that he allowed his wife to persuade him not to take notes.

He had a touching belief to the very end in 'resolutionary Christianity', and a great commitment to documentation. Thus, although his chief contribution to the ecumenical movement was certainly on its Life and Work side, he gave invaluable service to the actual quest for reunion by gathering together and editing with impeccable attention to detail four series of *Documents on Christian Unity*. The first series appeared in 1924, the fourth in 1958, the year of his death. They gathered together material much of which would otherwise only have been found in obscure and sometimes ephemeral publications. In the introduction to the last volume a characteristic note of optimism appeared. 'There is beyond doubt need for a much greater sense of urgency on all sides; and there have been various disappointments and checks. But students of the whole period 1920–58 cannot fail to receive an impression of a real movement forward. The goal is the restoration of unity to the whole Church of Christ.'[8]

For that unity, as well as for co-operation in witness, service and international friendship, Bell laboured hard. He was never content to be an ecumenist at the world level. Much of what was done at that level was judged its by relevance to Sussex. It was highly characteristic that on the Sunday of the Chichester meeting of the central committee in 1949 the members found themselves despatched to the pulpits of local churches to explain what it was all about. He was a pioneer, too, in the creation of a county council of churches. The Sussex Council of Churches has now had twenty years of valuable life. It took its origin at a meeting called by Bell in 1951 to which he invited members of the diocesan missionary council together with some thirty representatives of the Free Churches. After the Evanston assembly there was a 'Sussex Evanston' in the form of a short residential conference. In his letter of invitation Bell wrote:

> It is of the greatest importance to secure that the ecumenical movement has its proper expression not only on the national but also on the local level. . . . The object of this Conference is both to help the members of the Conference to be better informed about the Evanston message, and most particularly to consider how Evanston and the ecumenical movement can be related to local conditions, and developed in a form agreeable to the Church of England and the Free Churches in our diocese.[9]

It was from this conference that, again at Bell's urging, the body arose which has been known since 1959 as the Sussex Council of Churches, which has enabled the coordination of much local work, the exchange of ideas and a considerable ecumenical interest to be stimulated. Local councils of churches were brought into being where none existed, and they and older councils were brought into conference for the advancement of their work. The Rev. B. R. H. Spaull, Free Church vice-chairman of the Sussex Council under Bell's chairmanship, particularly stresses the contribution brought about to Crawley New Town by the ecumenical appointment through the Sussex Council of an industrial chaplain, for whose salary Bell was chiefly responsible through his diocesan board of finance.

Had all world and national ecumenical leaders been as

determined not to leave their ecumenical commitment behind as they left their inter-church conferences and became absorbed in the demands of their day-to-day work, the whole story of Christian unity would have been markedly different.

Bell's was by no means a sentimental ecumenism. There was a tough element in his churchmanship as well as in his international witness. One young clergyman in the diocese who had to go to him to confess an action that had broken all the rules, says 'He had a healthy respect for rules.' Bell was silent for a moment or two, and then he said in tones of mixed incredulity and bewilderment, 'Why?' He was Davidson's man to the end.

Some Free Churchmen were surprised by what they felt was an illiberal interpretation by this deeply committed ecumenist of the rules regarding the interchange of pulpits in his diocese. Yet again, Dr Ernest Payne, the Baptist leader, who was to become so close a colleague in the World Council's work, did not expect as firm a line to be taken by Bell in dealing with a few Anglican clergy in his diocese who, under strong conservative evangelical influence, had sought believers' baptism and then sought to return to their Anglican allegiance. 'They must be disciplined,' was Bell's response.

Part of the reason for this was Bell's own catholic form of Anglican churchmanship; but part was related to his desire to introduce a greater order in the Church of England. His own struggle in his diocese was with Anglo-Catholic lawlessness. He would have opened himself to attack if he had seemed willing to play ducks and drakes with the rules at the other extreme or in the interests of his own ecumenical commitment.

Bell did not desire a vague inter-denominationalism, or a spiritual unity which did not seek structural expression. He yearned for a unity which would make divided churches one in their common life. This led him in the closing years of his life to give much of his energy to his chairmanship of the Anglican–Methodist conversations. His fellow chairman was the Methodist theologian, Dr Harold Roberts. Dr Roberts writes:

He brought to the commission a burning passion for Christian unity and a deep conviction that nothing need ultimately stand in the way of closer relations between the churches. He himself could best be described as a high churchman, but he so interpreted his own churchmanship as to awaken a desire among those nurtured in other traditions to share his inheritance. . . . It is true to say that even those who could not subscribe to his views on the nature of the ministry and sacraments felt that they did not wish to belong to a church from which he was excluded.[10]

It was at a meeting of the commission in April 1958 that he was found lying unconscious on the floor of his room. He seemed to make a good recovery, but it was the beginning of the end. He was in fact worn out. He managed to attend the Lambeth Conference in the summer, but he was mortally tired. He went on to the central committee of the World Council at Nyborg, Denmark. By then even in appearance he was not himself. When invited to give to the preliminary executive committee a short account of the visit that he had paid to Pope John in March, he spoke for an hour. Even then there were not lacking gleams of the old Bell. The Pope had said how good it was to meet him again. 'But we had never met before,' said Bell. 'But I could hardly tell him that,' he added with his shy smile.

On the Sunday during that meeting he preached what was to be his last sermon. It was in Odense, and only with difficulty was he virtually pushed up into the very high Lutheran pulpit. There came a long pause, distressing to all who knew his condition. Then in an unnaturally loud voice, he began to preach very slowly. It seemed almost consciously his spiritual last will and testament. He gave out his text, Luke 17.10, 'So likewise ye, when ye shall have done all those things which are commanded you, say, We are unprofitable servants: we have done that which was our duty to do.' His first words were, 'There is a stone in the floor of Uppsala Cathedral on which these words are inscribed. It is the gravestone of Archbishop Nathan Söderblom.' The service was to mark the tenth anniversary of the full formation of the World Council. Bell surveyed what had led up to that step and the needs which the future imposed. He made one final appeal. It was 'for more saintly lives'. He buttressed it with a quotation from his ecumenical master, Söderblom.

> When God's rule has penetrated man's heart and life so that the divine love and righteousness becomes the main factor we speak of a saint. A saint is one who reveals God's might. Saints are such as show clearly and plainly in their lives and deeds and in their very being that God lives.[11]

It was truly his last will and testament. It was also, in total humble unawareness, the description of the whole purpose of his own life. That life closed on 3 October 1958. At a memorial service which thronged St Martin-in-the-Fields some days later (in which Martin Niemöller shared) Dr Visser 't Hooft preached from the text Bell had chosen at Odense, and said as he closed:

> 'When you shall have done all these things, say we are unprofitable servants.' He has done all these things, simply, without making a noise about it, because he was in the service of a Master. He had not invented any of it. It was the Master who had lived and died for *all* men. The Master Himself had been the servant of the Lord and George Bell only followed him. But in doing so he has not only 'to the end persisting, safe arrived', but also helped us all to understand better what the service of the Lord Christ really means.[12]

NOTES

1. *The First Assembly of the World Council of Churches: Official Report*, ed. W. A. Visser 't Hooft, SCM Press 1949, p. 25.

2. Ibid., p. 102.

3. Review of Jasper, see ch. 1, fn. 11.

4. Letter to the author.

5. Kenneth Grubb, *Crypts of Power*, Hodder & Stoughton 1971, p. 172.

6. See *The Kingship of Christ*, pp. 89–91.

7. Letter to the author.

8. G. K. A. Bell, ed., *Documents on Christian Unity, Fourth Series 1948–57*, OUP 1958, p. xviii.

9. Memorandum supplied by the present Bishop of Chichester, Dr Roger Wilson.

10. Letter to the author.

11. The whole sermon is in *The Ecumenical Review*, Vol. XI, No. 1, October 1958.

12. The whole tribute is in *The Ecumenical Review*, Vol. XI, No. 2, January 1959.

7 'An Authentic Apostle'

When the war ended Bell stepped naturally and as of right into the world ecumenical leadership vacated by the death of William Temple. He had not stepped into the leadership of the Church of England and the whole Anglican communion which is given to the occupant of the see of Canterbury.

When Temple died in 1944 the Christian world reeled from the suddenness and shock of it. The same news caused a Tory member of Parliament to make this entry in his diary:

> The Archbishop was . . . a fat fool of 63 with a fuddled, muddled brain. . . . He was a Socialist, and Winston was much criticized for appointing him: now after 2½ years he can put that right.[1]

True, this was the reaction of the egregious 'Chips' Channon, but it indicates in brutal and almost mindlessly venomous form the reaction of some of those who felt threatened by Temple's advocacy of more equitable social policies. The existence of a swathe of opinion of that type amongst those who exerted much influence cannot be ignored when the question is examined, 'Was Bell of Chichester deliberately passed over when Temple died?' Involved in this is the very serious issue whether the present form of Crown appointment to leadership in the national church excludes the true prophet.

Some, like Professor Donald Mackinnon, make no bones about the tragedy they see to be involved in the failure to appoint Bell.

The historians of the Church of England may yet recognize that the worst misfortune to befall its leadership in the end of the war was less the premature death of William Temple than his succession by Fisher of London, and not by Bell of Chichester.[2]

This is, of course, a value-judgment – that Bell would have made a better archbishop than Fisher. With that we have no immediate concern, save in so far as such a judgment sheds light upon our subject. Our concern with this question is whether Bell was of such outstanding ability, achievement and character that he could only have been passed over because influential persons were determined that a man who bore his kind of witness should be excluded from the place of chief ecclesiastical leadership.

The case must be judged 'not proven'. There is now fairly strong evidence that Bell was considered, or rather his name was laid before Churchill by Halifax, who had been firmly tackled on the subject by his friend Father E. K. Talbot.[3] It is certain that there were those in the Church of England who felt that his claim was unmatched by that of any other. His deep knowledge of the work of Lambeth, gained by his apprenticeship to Davidson and by his work upon Davidson's biography, together with the leadership he had shown among the churches of Europe and his effectiveness and seniority as a diocesan bishop seemed to such judges to raise him above the level of his fellow bishops. No man could be fully Temple's heir, but Bell looked more likely to continue his work than anybody else. Even the controversies in which he had become involved showed his capacity for an informed Christian leadership which concentrated on the matters that should really be concerning men of faith.

But if there was disappointment amongst some who made this judgment, and even anger that the Crown's advisers could seem vindictive in excluding one so evidently equipped

113

because of the testimony he had borne for righteousness, there was not the beginning of a public outcry. We can imagine what would have happened if Churchill had not appointed Temple in 1942. Temple's biographer has revealed that Temple himself doubted whether at that moment in the war the 'powers' would select him for Canterbury, yet he adds:

> But it was impossible to pass him over. It is safe to say that, under any system of election or appointment, by Church or State or both, the choice would have fallen on Temple.[4]

In this sense it was possible to pass Bell over in 1944, because not even his most fervent admirer would have classed his gifts with those of Temple. There was furthermore a greater temptation to pass him over for those who had quarrelled with Temple's Christian concern with the whole range of social, economic and political life. The very fact that there had been a Temple made it more difficult for the 'establishment' to nominate a Bell.

But the question must arise whether he had not in fact been passed over some years before. There is clear evidence that Temple expected Fisher of London to succeed him at Canterbury (as he had long before succeeded him at Repton). He had remarked to his wife that he must give up 'in time to let Geoffrey have his whack'.[5] Obviously then he was contemplating retirement, not his death before the year was out. But Bell was only four years Fisher's senior, and it is striking (and too little noted in the various discussions of the succession to the primacy in 1944) that Temple saw Fisher as the next Archbishop of Canterbury.

Adrian Carey, chaplain to Bell in some of the later years of his time at Chichester, writes: 'My own view is that if George Bell had been destined for Lambeth, he *must* have been translated to London when Winnington Ingram

114

retired. From that moment (long before the war speeches) Geoffrey Fisher was the heir apparent.'[6] Garbett's biographer, Canon Charles Smyth, also reveals that, away in India in 1938, on seeing the news that A. T. P. Williams was going to be Bishop of Durham, both Garbett and his chaplain interpreted it as definitely meaning that Fisher would move to London (known to be coming vacant after the long reign of Winnington Ingram).[7] Although unknown to the public at large, Fisher as Bishop of Chester had enormously impressed those who had seen him at work, and he proved to have the precise combination of qualities which enabled the disorder of the London diocese to be cleared up without public dissension.

In fact, so far as the biographies reveal, the name of Bell was curiously absent from discussion when the pre-eminent sees came to be filled. There is no evidence that Temple struggled to have his ecumenical partner as his fellow-archbishop at York, or at least translated to Winchester when Garbett was preferred to Bishopthorpe. Bishop Barry can write that the choice of his friend Mervyn Haigh for Winchester at that time 'meant that George Bell was again being passed over'. He adds that this 'in itself was nothing short of scandalous, even though no advancement in the hierarchy could have added a cubit to Bell's moral stature'.[8] But if it was scandalous, it was a far from open scandal, and it certainly preceded the war-time speeches on obliteration bombing. In fact the government which had failed to nominate him to York or Winchester chose him some weeks later to represent his country to the churches of neutral Sweden.

It is in fact chiefly in retrospect, save to the most discerning, that the passing over of Bell seems strange. At the time, in 1944 when Temple died, and even in 1939 when London fell vacant or in 1942 when Lang's retirement brought about a general post, Bell's pre-eminent claims to occupy an unmistakable place in the central leadership of the Church of England were not so immediately obvious.

To recognize this is to focus attention on what is our particular concern. What was the actual character of this man who looms larger as the years go by, but who could fairly easily be passed over for the highest offices of his church? That he was an outstanding leader, or perhaps more precisely a farseeing prophet of God, the preceding pages should have made plain. But was George Kennedy Allen Bell a great man?

Certain attributes which enhance a man in the public mind, and make it difficult to ignore or pass over him, were in fact conspicuously missing. He was a speaker of almost overpowering dullness. I spoke with him at public meetings in Brighton both before and after the Evanston assembly. Here he was in the principal town of his diocese, speaking on both occasions in a crowded hall with people of all churches obviously going out in spirit towards him in evident affection. He had as his theme that manifestation of the world church which most passionately kindled his spirit; and he failed to give a moment's vividness to the significance of the occasion, whether speaking of Evanston in prospect or retrospect.

Partly it was the plain absence of the gift of eloquence; but partly, too, it was the defect of a quality. All the multitudinous concerns of his life never effaced the disciplined habits of the Lambeth years. Still he mastered his brief, and mastered it in depth. Whatever he was to speak about – and the range covered in his speeches is remarkable – he had to grasp fully, so that his facts were beyond challenge. If the issue was political his chaplain would have to help him ransack *Hansard* late at night; if it was theological he would seek advice and then read the best

116

big book on the subject. (Dr Harold Roberts recalls his enquiry regarding the Methodist doctrine of Christian perfection, and his securing of the weighty work on the theme by a German writer that was recommended to him – and reading it before they next met.) It is rare that such habits of industry can be formed and maintained without some crushing of the power to stimulate and refresh by speech and writing. Even allowing for the speed at which *The Kingship of Christ* (published as a Penguin Special) had to be written, it is sad to reflect that the author of that dull book once had the felicitous pen that wrote *Randall Davidson*. A dust of dullness settled on many of Bell's speeches because he worked too hard.

The same habit of industry led to the overloading of his speeches with fact and quotation. As Archbishop Lord Fisher gaily remarks of an occasion when they both spoke on the Federation of Rhodesia and Nyasaland in the Lords, 'There is another point in the contrast between our speeches. He always showed how deeply he had studied the question: his speech was carefully documented and in consequence lost in effectiveness.'[9]

Again and again in reminiscences there come references to the dulling effect of this habit on his speeches. Bishop Leslie Hunter remembers that they had a great respect for him in the House of Lords, for they admired both his courage and his integrity. 'He would, however, have been much more persuasive if his speeches had not been too overloaded with facts. He was not a good speaker.'[10] Bell had the fatal inability to make righteousness interesting. Assemblies such as the House of Lords might not complain that bishops preached in their speeches, but when with Bell the determination of a lecturer to instruct was added to the boring exhortation of the preacher it must have been hard to bear.

He had no power to kindle an audience, and his intense

shyness, which (as has been noted) made him wonder whether he could face the inevitable public social occasions involved in being chaplain at Lambeth, never left him. He was a man of long silences, and of no gregariousness. It would have been grotesque to imagine him sitting with some cronies swopping stories. Some have even doubted whether he had a sense of humour, but Adrian Carey, who as chaplain shared his life and his home, says that he could be full of reminiscences which showed his gaiety and impish wit. A certain slow and almost sly humour went with his shyness. When conversation had flowed very freely at the breakfast table when Mrs Bell's brother and sister-in-law, Sir Richard and Lady Livingstone, were visiting Chichester, the bishop was subject to wifely rebuke: 'George, you haven't said a word the whole of breakfast.' 'No, dear', came the gentle reply, 'there's been no need.' And when Hetty Bell appealed for George's support for her version of a story about William Temple when she had heard someone else tell the story rather differently, all she received was, 'Yes, dear. And I've heard you tell it rather differently.'

There was nothing chilly about Bell's shyness. No one would have been tempted to dub him, as his successor as Davidson's chaplain, Haigh, was dubbed, 'the holy icicle'. The dogged habit of work, and a natural quietness, did not mean any absence of warmth. He was in the full sense of the word a loving man, never tempted to care about causes and be careless of individuals. He had great natural dignity, and cared about the dignity of his office not in any prelatical way but as one whose habits and approach had been formed in a day with more assured sense of hierarchy and position. He was a very disciplined man himself, and found it hard to understand that others should be indisciplined.

The question is bound to arise whether discipline, industry, application and unceasing hard work are the ingredients that produce a prophet. Is not a prophet the man who is caught up by an almost disordered inspiration, the man whose life may lie fallow and unoccupied until suddenly the divine afflatus fills the emptiness of his days? Further, is not the prophet the man of unmistakable charismatic personality, so that in some almost unanalysable way people are swayed by him?

By such tests Bell fails; but are they legitimate tests and, above all, are they the relevant tests for today? He was not a charismatic personality as, in very contrasted ways, Pope John and Martin Luther King were. This gravely limited his public impact, and to the degree that that was limited it became easier to avoid the challenge that would have come from giving him one of the primacies or, say, the bishopric of London. But if he was not charismatic in public influence and acclaim there can be no doubt that he had a remarkable personal charisma. This appears unmistakably in his relationship with Dietrich Bonhoeffer.

The Bonhoeffer now revealed in the large biographies and in the volumes of his papers is a man always tempted towards intellectual pride and arrogance. To realize this is to appreciate more fully the beauty of character that appears almost throughout the *Letters and Papers from Prison*, the first medium through which most people came to know him. He had a particular detestation for the Anglo-Saxon pelagianism in religion that he encountered during his visits to the USA, and for the easy theological liberalism that still held sway in England during the 1930s. Bonhoeffer was the dialectical and biblical theologian through and through, and had a characteristically Teutonic contempt for what was not intellectually rigorous and profound. It was only to Barth among theologians that he granted real authority over him, as Bethge noted; and Barth was a giant.

But, as Bethge also noted, he gave real authority over himself to Bell of Chichester. Barth and Bell alone commanded this allegiance. Bell was certainly no giant in theology: what, then, was it about this gentle, very English bishop that held in thrall the young German theologian and martyr who has become perhaps the greatest Christian hero of the post-war world? If we could fully penetrate that secret we should know what the charisma was which gave to Bell a real, if unusual, measure of greatness.

Part of it, certainly, was the plain power of a man whose life was hid with Christ in God. Bonhoeffer came from a family that was virtually agnostic, and somewhat startled them by his resolve to be a theologian and minister. It was in large measure an intellectual commitment. Starting from that point, the devotional life of Catholic Anglicanism came to fascinate him, and the result of visits to Kelham and Mirfield was the introduction of the practice of meditation into the secret Confessing Church seminary at Finkelwalde (not without some opposition from his bewildered students). It is clear that Bonhoeffer saw in Bell a power of the spirit that was nurtured by his use of the means of grace. It was this as much as anything that caused him to yield a spiritual authority to his Anglican father-in-God comparable with the intellectual authority that he gave to Karl Barth.

This power of the spirit did not stand alone in that relationship, although it must have illuminated for the brilliant young theologian how pride and arrogance might be subjected to Christ. Another element was the intensity of Bell's sympathy. The word compassion can be lightly used in these days when Christian service is exalted to be the heart of discipleship. For Bell it had its original meaning of a 'suffering with'. He was not just interested in the German church struggle: he agonized with those who were caught up in it. He was not just desirous of helping the non-Aryan refugee or the interned Germans in 1940: he felt their misery and brought to his efforts to relieve them a passionate commitment. Twenty-six years after his visit to the internment camp in the Isle of Man a woman wrote of him:

> He listened with patience and understanding. Thus he became for us (on our island) a bridge (physically and spiritually) to the world at large, in reality and humanity.[11]

She added that his visit was an unforgettable experience.

When more than a quarter of a century later someone is moved to write about him, just because his voice was heard again in a radio programme, the words 'unforgettable experience' are delivered from platitude. This hesitant man, with no vestige of easy camaraderie, by just sitting and listening to people in desperation brought them immense succour. It was something of the same power that drew Bonhoeffer to him as he faced the soiling of his fatherland and the near destruction of the church by the Hitler regime.

There is an instructive contrast between the power of this listening man, sitting quietly, with his prominent and bright blue eyes steadily fixed on the person pouring out his need, and the seeming inefficacy of the same man trying to bring home to some assembly by a speech the moral challenge of the hour. Suffering men speak of Bell's compassion and sympathy: challenged men speak of his obstinacy and ill-timed pertinacity.

It seems clear that he was not always tactically skilful. He did not have the power to insinuate his ideas into the minds of his hearers; he certainly had no skill in stepping backwards in order to leap forward the better. He seemed to begin from a fixed and obdurate position, and some in the Lords complained that he had the power of inflaming the issues that he touched. The very degree to which he had done his 'home-work' could be off-putting. (I recall

121

an occasion when he had introduced a resolution on megaton weapons at a meeting of the British Council of Churches. The Archbishop of Canterbury said he did not know what the word meant, whereupon his brother of Chichester expounded the word with a saintly forbearance towards almost invincible ignorance that must have been needlessly trying to the former Headmaster of Repton.)

There was nevertheless more than tactical failure underlying the constant accusation of an unwise pertinacity. The combination of such remarkable and wide-ranging industry with deep devotional habit was bound to produce an almost dangerous measure of conviction in his mind. Archbishop Lord Fisher comments on his vast knowledge of what had happened in the past in the Church of England and his resource in accumulating documentary evidence; and adds:

> So equipped, he generally had in his mind the solution to any question before it was debated, and the solution thought out in great detail. This he would work for, and if he was unsuccessful, he would often 'go underground' and still keep it among his active purposes, and, as soon as he saw an opportunity a year, or two, or three years later, up it would come again. This was a characteristic of his that we all knew. One could never be sure that George Bell had dropped an idea for which he had failed to win general approval.[12]

The defect of his spiritual and industrious qualities was a real one, and combined with his lack of eloquence and his shyness probably enabled him to be disregarded by those responsible for the higher appointments in the Church of England. We may feel with Bishop Barry that no advancement in the hierarchy would have added a cubit to his moral stature, but it seems clear that Bell felt that his being left in Chichester was a deliberate decision not to advance one who had irritated what Temple called the 'powers'. David Edwards comments; 'His lack of luck in the gamble of promotion would scarcely be worth mentioning (for being the senior clergyman in Sussex cannot be martyrdom) had not this teacher of Dietrich Bonhoeffer been also the disciple of Randall Davidson, thoroughly aware of England's established conventions – and rewards.'[13]

Even when he was seventy he proved willing to allow his name to be pressed by Archbishops Garbett and Fisher for nomination to York on the former's retirement. Archdeacon Mason says that 'he privately hoped that this appointment might be regarded as something of a vindication of his speeches during the war'. He heard no more about it, and then learned of Dr Michael Ramsey's translation to York on the radio.[14]

It would probably have been unwise to nominate a man of seventy to succeed an octogenarian whose powers had suffered a sad and sudden failure in the closing period, but the two Archbishops' desire to bring his name forward even at the age of seventy is a measure of their recognition of his stature. Nor can age have been the only barrier to nomination, for even when Bell announced his retirement from his see and his old friend of the university settlement days, F. J. Marquis, now Lord Woolton, on behalf of a company of friends, privately urged the government to confer some notable honour such as the Companionship of Honour upon him, the only answer was silence.[15] If Bell had been too pertinacious and obdurate in his pleading for humanity in war, there were some in the governing élite of this country who remained too vindictive and mean to honour a greatness of heart and spirit that had been acclaimed throughout the Christian world.

For, when every qualification has been made concerning the defects of his qualities and the occasional tactical unwisdom of his tenacity, it remains true that his gravest offence was that he made men uncomfortable by his unyielding proclamation of righteousness. Much is self-gratifyingly made of the English talent for tolerantly honouring the man who has made an unpopular stand; but there is another and darker tradition. It is that of an implacable refusal to forgive the man who has betrayed the 'establishment' from within. That was Bell's offence, and it was to the end unpardonable. He who had been the confidential chaplain and alter ego of the most trusted archbishop ever to tread the carpet of the Athenaeum or draw statesmen into his room at the Lords, and had himself moved with ease and confidence amidst the instruments of establishment power, the Upper House of Convocation, the columns of *The Times*, the House of Lords and the Athenaeum itself, had allowed his German obsession to overthrow his judgment and even his loyalty.

It was in fact in regard to Germany, both before and during the war, that he earned the title which Professor Donald Mackinnon has given to him, 'an authentic apostle'.[16] Before the war he saw that Nazism represented not a temporary excess in an essential move to hold back Bolshevism (as so many in the governing élite saw it), but an evil which in subtler and therefore more dangerous ways would destroy the spiritual life of man. During the war he saw that the years of attrition were gradually leading to assimilation to the dehumanized brutality that supposedly was being fought. Against Nazism and against the way that Nazism finally came to be fought he raised up the voice of a gentle but implacable prophet. George Kennedy Allen Bell was a great man because he saw to the heart of the dilemma of our century, and he did it almost despite the whole temper of his own training and formation.

In the end it was not Davidson's Bell but Söderblom's Bell that remained. The techniques forged under Davidson were used to the close of Bell's life; the careful investigation, the painstaking documentation, the interrogation of the expert. The instruments of influence used by Davidson were grasped by his former chaplain; but the vision was that of the other archbishop who kindled Bell's slow but steady fire. It was the vision of a church that transcended nationality even in time of war, and a church which proclaimed a care for humanity without which victory would be a hollow farce. Davidson lived secure in a Constantinian concordat between church and state: Bell, perhaps almost unconsciously but driven to it by simple Christian obedience, faced the fact that the church had entered the post-Constantinian era. The measure of Bell's greatness was the degree to which he obeyed the plain demands of discipleship in his day, untrammelled by the restraints of his own background. His prophetic vision came in no ecstatic way, but in the twentieth-century fashion of consultation and conference; but to the dialogue of such gatherings Bell took the fruit of another dialogue. It was the dialogue between God and his own spirit. From that dialogue came the power to see the tasks of a Christian leader in the middle of our turbulent century, and from it, too, came the power to do them with that dogged and unswerving tenacity which the world will often call obstinacy, but Christian men will call consecration.

It was after the Stockholm conference, when Bell was still the young Dean of Canterbury, that Söderblom wrote to Davidson, 'This Bell never rings for nothing.'[17] He has not stopped ringing yet.

NOTES

1. Robert Rhodes James (ed.), *Chips: The Diaries of Sir Henry Channon*, Wiedenfeld & Nicolson 1967, p. 396.
2. Quoted by Roger Lloyd, *The Church of England 1900–1965*, SCM Press 1966, pp. 463–464. Canon Lloyd's discussion of the point is very interesting.
3. Letter in *Crucible* already quoted.

4. F. A. Iremonger, *William Temple*, OUP 1948, pp. 474–475.

5. Ibid., p. 620.

6. Letter to the author.

7. *Cyril Forster Garbett*, p. 238.

8. *Mervyn Haigh*, p. 142.

9. Letter to the author.

10. Letter to the author.

11. Janet Lacey, *A Cup of Water*, Hodder & Stoughton 1970, p. 75.

12. William Purcell, *Fisher of Lambeth*, Hodder & Stoughton 1969, p. 99.

13. David L. Edwards, *Leaders of the Church of England*, OUP 1971, pp. 339–340.

14 and 15. Article in *Crucible* already quoted.

16. See a broadcast talk published in *The Listener*, 21 December 1967, and in extended form in *The Stripping of the Altars*, Collins Fontana Books 1969, pp. 83–92. I am indebted to Professor Mackinnon for the 'post-Constantinian era' point.

17. Bethge, p. 288.